To

_____

From

_____

Date

_____

100 Great Ideas to Simplify Your Life

Tyndale House Publishers, Inc.
Carol Stream, Illinois

Visit Tyndale's exciting Web site at www.tyndale.com.

TYNDALE and Tyndale's quill logo are registered trademarks of Tyndale House Publishers, Inc.

100 Great Ideas to Simplify Your Life
Copyright © 2011 by GRQ, Inc. All rights reserved.

Writer: Candy Paull
Editor: Teri K. Wilhelms
Design: Whisner Design Group

Library of Congress Cataloging-in-Publication Data
Paull, Candy.
  100 great ideas to simplify your life / [writer, Candy Paull].
     p. cm.
  Includes bibliographical references.
  ISBN 978-1-4143-3886-6 (sc)
  1. Simplicity—Religious aspects—Christianity. I. Title.
  BV4647.S48P38 2011
  241'.4—dc22
                          2010024015

Printed in the United States of America

ISBN 978-1-4143-3886-6

16 15 14 13 12 11 10
  7   6   5   4   3   2   1

A pretentious, showy life is an empty life;
a plain and simple life is a full life.

Proverbs 13:7, THE MESSAGE

Be an example to all believers in what you say, in the way you live,
in your love, your faith, and your purity.

1 Timothy 4:12, NLT

Purity and simplicity are the two wings with which man
soars above the earth and all temporary nature.

Thomas à Kempis

Strive first for the kingdom of God and his righteousness,
and all these things will be given to you as well.

Matthew 6:33, NRSV

If any of you lacks wisdom, let him ask of God, who gives to
all liberally and without reproach, and it will be given to him.

James 1:5, NKJV

Contents

Contents continued

Trust and Faith

Material Wealth

Contents continued

Contents continued

Prayer and Presence

Harmony and Order

Do not boast about tomorrow, for you do not know what a day may bring forth.

Proverbs 27:1, NIV

*There are many activities I must cut out simply because
I desire to excel in my pursuit after God and holiness.*

Wendell W. Price

*The LORD will guide you continually,
and satisfy your soul in drought,
and strengthen your bones;
you shall be like a watered garden,
and like a spring of water, whose waters do not fail.*

Isaiah 58:11, NKJV

*It's a mistake to look too far ahead. Only one link in
the chain of destiny can be handled at a time.*

Sir Winston Churchill

The Lord is the Spirit, and wherever the Spirit of the Lord is, there is freedom.

2 Corinthians 3:17, NLT

Introduction

Simplicity, clarity, singleness: These are the attributes that give our lives
power and vividness and joy as they are also the marks of great art.
They seem to be the purpose of God for his whole creation.

Richard Holloway

True simplicity involves more than clearing the clutter from your home, making do with less, or organizing your outer life more efficiently. Authentic simplicity is a radical spiritual choice. It is a choice to move out of the frenetic pace of an ever-accelerating and ever-accumulating worldview into a life lived more in harmony with the priorities of God's Kingdom.

The simplicity of paring down, cleaning out, and clearing clutter in your physical life can be a reflection of an inner simplicity that is deeply rooted in God. This inner spiritual simplicity can be described as a childlike faith in the one who created you and who is with you every single day of your life.

The great ideas of a simpler life may seem small and unimportant at first glance, but these ideas are like seeds planted in the mind and the heart. Choosing silence over media distraction, emphasizing loving relationships above monetary calculations, and becoming a contributor to life instead of merely being a consumer are all ways you can create a life you truly love. Let these simple and practical meditations remind you that no matter how crazy life can feel, there is sweet, slow sanity waiting at the center of your being, hidden in the heart of God.

Choosing simplicity is choosing to live in concert with divine priorities. Even the smallest act of living more simply will help you savor your one precious life and see God's grace unfolding in every moment of your day.

We prove ourselves by our purity, our understanding, our patience, our kindness,
by the Holy Spirit within us, and by our sincere love.

2 Corinthians 6:6, NLT

1

Walk in Simple Faith

*You will keep in
perfect peace all
who trust in you,
all whose thoughts
are fixed on you!*

Isaiah 26:3, NLT

Move beyond the worship of success and the values of consumerism to embrace a simpler life. Embrace a more mindful way of living that invites a sense of spirituality in all you do. From buying less to sharing more generously, simplifying your life is about wedding your spiritual values with your daily life.

Start with your schedule. Are you so busy you don't have time to breathe? If you don't have time for the important things in life, like being with loved ones or making time to be alone with God, something needs to change. Assess how you spend your money. One simple step could be to forgo a purchase and save money.

Does the way you live your life match your spiritual ideals? You don't have to make giant leaps of faith. Baby steps will do. One step leads to another, and each choice you make to simplify your life builds on the last. A simple faith in God leads you along gently, one step of faith at a time.

Make one simple decision and see where it takes you. Ask for God's guidance. Be especially mindful of the small choices that can have a big impact over the long term.

Redefine Success

2

How do you define success? Money? Education? Good looks? Social standing? How you appear to others? If you've been feeling as if you don't measure up, maybe you need to redefine what success means to you. The simple life is lived with a different set of values.

Cultivate an image of success that presents a warmer, more human appearance. Success can be found in raising a healthy family, serving your community, creating a welcoming home, encouraging friends, or simply doing your best every day. Measure your life by a different standard, one that satisfies the heart. Sometimes that will include a plainer lifestyle, avoiding the conspicuous consumption the world demands.

Focus on God's priorities instead of the world's image of success. Do your best, and trust God with the rest. There is no one-size-fits-all formula for success. True success is a life well lived, in harmony with God, others, and yourself. Be assured that if you define success as seeking God first, you will never be a failure.

Make a list of successes you would like to achieve. Pray about the list. Get together with friends and share stories of things that looked like failures but turned into unexpected blessings and success.

Your success and happiness lie in you. External conditions are the accidents of life, its outer trappings. The great, enduring realities are love and service.

Helen Keller

3

Fix What's Broken

*Commit your works
to the LORD, and
your thoughts will
be established.*

Proverbs 16:3, NKJV

Your car needs a tune-up. You have a stack of mending to do. You will expend less energy fixing the car and doing the mending than you will avoiding the work or beating yourself up for not doing what needs to be done. A door that moves easily on its hinges, a car that runs smoothly, and buttons sewed on properly make life not only simpler but also more pleasant.

You feel satisfied when everything works harmoniously, functioning in order and ease. You feel better about yourself as well. Fixing what is broken is a form of committing to your own good, which then frees you to put your energy into creating a happier and more meaningful life.

Sometimes relationships need patching up. Take the time and effort to rebuild those bridges you've burned. Listen to your heart's instinct for healing a wounded relationship. Ask God to show you the best way to heal the wounds. Right wrongs when you can, and forgive the rest. Trust that all things will be restored with divine timing and grace.

*Set aside some things that need mending. Reserve a quiet
evening or weekend afternoon to tackle at least one of the
items in the pile. Enjoy the satisfaction of creating order
and harmony as you make something useful again.*

Persevere in Tough Times

4

Losses, layoffs, deaths, sudden changes—life takes its toll and you begin to be afraid that the road of life has turned into a dark and dangerous dead end. Unexpected detours happen. Tough times have their seasons. But the seasons change, and what you thought was the end of the road may turn out to be only a bend in the road.

Any worthwhile plan changes and evolves. Do the work. Realize that it may take longer than you had planned. Remember that every detour and delay can be an opportunity to examine your priorities and get clear on what is truly important to you. This could be a time to simplify your life by eliminating distractions that hold you back.

When you feel overwhelmed, take time to nurture your relationship with God. Persevere and trust that his strength sustains you through every trouble and trial, and through all the changes of a lifetime. Rely on this inner strength to help you deal with the challenges of daily life.

Do not cast away your confidence, which has great reward. For you have need of endurance, so that after you have done the will of God, you may receive the promise.

Hebrews 10:35-36, NKJV

Spend time with people who are hopeful, helpful, and encouraging. Reach out to a friend who is struggling. Tell each other stories of times when God was faithful, and pray together as you go through tough times now.

5 Create Heaven on Earth

Be grateful for the blessings you enjoy—God has enriched your life with more than you need. Savor the simple things that make life worth living, and remember to share your surplus with others. This is one way to bring the Kingdom of Heaven to earth.

One particularly effective way to create a taste of heaven on earth is to clear your living space of clutter, creating an atmosphere of peaceful calm instead of chaos and disorder. As you clean and clear, decide what you want to keep and where you want to keep it. Just as comfortable and flattering clothing makes you feel your best, so beauty and order in your home will lift your spirits.

Clearing emotional clutter will also help you live life more freely from the heart. As you allow God to bring peace to your heart, you'll begin to experience more of the sweet serenity that comes through the fruit of the Spirit. Give thanks for the small joys of living simply in God's abundant and loving providence.

Start with one room in your home: weed out the clutter and leave only those things that are meaningful, useful, or beautiful. Ask yourself: Is it beautiful? Can I use this? Do I need it?

Stick to the Basics

6

Your mom started you on the basics: Pick up your toys. Wash behind your ears. Play nicely together. Your life as an adult got more complicated and acquisitive. Now it's time to get back to the basics by moving beyond the more-means-happiness myth. Make your life less complex and cluttered so you can enjoy a more authentic life.

Start by clarifying your values and setting priorities. Ask yourself how you can live more simply and meaningfully. Look for ways you can become more self-sufficient. Do you really need to buy fancy prepackaged meals? Instead, make healthy home-cooked meals. Organize your household, plan ahead, clear clutter, and be kind to yourself and to others— these are some of the basics you always need to practice.

Practice the spiritual basics, too, because sophisticated theories are no substitute for living in the light of faith, hope, and love. There is no substitute for the consistent practice of faith in daily life. Keep in mind that practicing the basics well will affect every aspect of your life in positive ways.

A little knowledge of God is worth more than a great deal of knowledge about him.

J. I. Packer

Create a personal mission statement. Include practical ways you intend to express God's love in the world. Write a simple affirmation based on your mission statement. Post it on your refrigerator as a reminder.

7

Ask Better Questions

*The mind is good—
God put it there. He
gave us our heads and
it was not his intention
that our heads would
function just as a place
to hang a hat.*

A. W. Tozer

Sometimes asking the right question can lead you to an unexpected and more empowering answer. If you're looking for better options, ask questions that will generate solutions that take you out of the box and into a more expansive viewpoint.

Begin by asking basic questions. Ask yourself: *Does this choice simplify or complicate my life?* and *How will this choice help me live according to spiritual values?* For example, instead of looking in a mirror and asking, *Does this outfit make me look fat?* ask questions that emphasize a more positive view, such as, *Does this make me feel comfortable and confident?* or *Will others feel at ease around me?* If you are uncomfortable or self-conscious about what you choose to wear, you will end up focusing on your discomfort instead of feeling free to concentrate on enjoying life and helping others.

Another classic question has helped many make wiser decisions and find better solutions. Ask yourself, *What would Jesus do?* Asking better questions can lead to elegant solutions and profound insight.

*Make notes on questions you have with a problem or issue.
Now look at your questions and see if they are limiting
you to old answers. Imagine more creative
questions that will inspire new ideas.*

Claim the Blessing

8

One night Jacob had an encounter with the Lord by the banks of the river Jabbok. Genesis 32:24 states that a man came and wrestled with him until daybreak. Jacob claimed he saw God face-to-face in that encounter, and he would not let his opponent go until he blessed him.

Sometimes life can feel like a wrestling match. There's that pile of papers that keeps growing, an increasingly demanding schedule, a complex situation involving a relationship, or a struggle with your own fears and failures. When the complexities of a challenging situation make you feel as if you are wrestling for your life, remember Jacob.

Hold on tight, look for God's presence in your situation, and claim the hidden blessing with a strong and simple faith. The chaos and confusion of life may wrestle you to the ground, but always know there is a blessing to be found in every situation. Know that the love of God is stronger than death and greater than all the challenges life can throw at you.

Jacob replied, "I will not let you go unless you bless me."

Genesis 32:26, NIV

Think about a difficulty you have been wrestling with and the potential blessings that might grow from this challenging situation. Give thanks in prayer that even if you don't understand how, hidden blessings will one day be revealed.

9

Strengthen Your Creative Muscles

Don't be impressed with yourself. Don't compare yourself with others. Each of you must take responsibility for doing the creative best you can with your own life.

Galatians 6:4-5,
THE MESSAGE

It takes creativity to live the simple life. You need discipline and ingenuity to move from chaos into order and harmony. You've got to develop creative muscle to move mountains. Creative muscles must be used, or they will atrophy.

Creativity begins with an idea. It might be a better way to stretch a dollar or a more artful approach to beautifying your home. Play with ideas and give your imagination room to roam. Allowing ourselves to be creative reflects the Creator's nature in our human nature. We were born creative.

There are no "wrong" answers in the creative process. Don't let perfectionism keep you from creating. Process, not product, is the point of any creative activity. Often it is the "mistakes" that lead to a new way of seeing, a new way of approaching our work.

Set aside time to nurture your creativity. Build skills with simple daily repetition. "Practice makes perfect" may be an old cliché, but it is still true. God was pleased with his creation of the world as chronicled in Genesis. Allowing ourselves to be creative reflects a similar joy in our divine creativity.

List twenty things you enjoy doing. Do one small creative activity today. Take pleasure in what you do, knowing that the act of creation can enhance your serenity and inspire a more focused approach to life.

Follow Your Heart

10

The heart is wiser than the head. When a complex decision arises, the heart finds the simplest and most elegant answers. When it comes to the most important choices in life, the wisdom of the heart guides you with grace. For example, the most logical choice in a career might seem to be the big-money job, but you'll find more satisfaction in doing something you love, even though it might mean less money. When it's a choice between love and logic, let love be the deciding factor.

Instead of buying extravagant things, be extravagant with your love. Cherish those who are dear to your heart. Invest time in building lasting, loving relationships. Remember that people are more important than things, and only love lasts beyond the grave.

When you let your heart lead the way, you'll discover that you've tapped into God's highest wisdom. God is love, and when you make choices out of love, you align yourself with his priorities. Trust love to lead you in the right direction.

We are shaped and fashioned by what we love.

Johann Wolfgang von Goethe

Focus on something that makes you happy to be who you are.
Evaluate your present goals. Are they consistent with
your innate gifts and talents? Do you see them
as fulfilling God's purposes for your life?

11

Learn to Listen

The heart of the discerning acquires knowledge; the ears of the wise seek it out.

Proverbs 18:15, NIV

A couple converses at a table in a restaurant. A breeze whispers through the branches of a tree by your window. Cicadas sing under a summer moon. A fountain creates a trickle of cooling music. You live in a sea of sound. Whether the sounds are beautiful or unpleasant, they offer a sound track that enriches your life.

Listening is a skill you can develop. If you've been walking around deaf to the wonder of the world you live in, you'll find that learning to listen will make your life richer—without spending a penny. It's as free as air.

Listening better will also help you make wiser decisions. Whether it's hearing an essential detail in a business conversation or being aware that your nearest and dearest wants to tell you something important, listening better facilitates and simplifies communication.

When you train yourself to listen to life, you'll discover that you've also learned to listen to God in a new way. Let the wonder of sound teach you lessons about listening to God.

Close your eyes and listen to the sounds that surround you. How do these sounds enrich your love of life and God's creation? Think about the last conversation you shared. Did you really listen? How can you become a better listener?

Believe in Yourself

12

It takes courage to simplify your life. You have to believe in yourself enough to make the tough decisions. You have to be brave enough and want it enough to say no to old habits that hold you back, and to say yes to learning new skills that will help you create a more balanced and fulfilling life.

Believe in yourself. Give yourself credit for the victories won. Give yourself grace for the losses and setbacks. Calm confidence from within reflects in your outer life. Knowing that God is with you every step of the way, believe that you can achieve your goals, overcome your difficulties, and fulfill your unique destiny. When you have faith in yourself, then others will believe in you, too, and support you as you reach for your dreams.

If you cherish a dream in your heart, you've got to give it your best shot. You'll never know if you don't try. Trust God to open the doors of opportunity. And then be brave enough to walk through them.

Ask in faith, never doubting, for the one who doubts is like a wave of the sea, driven and tossed by the wind.

James 1:6, NRSV

Think of all the activities you take part in during a typical week. Consider what those activities say about your approach to success. Ask God which activities could be dropped from your schedule in order to simplify your life.

Making Wise Choices

*The heart is wiser than the head. Though you need to pay attention to the
logic of the mind, when it comes to the most important choices in life,
the wisdom of the heart is your best guide. Ask, and God will give
you the wisdom to know what to do and when to do it.*

Wisdom is the knowledge and ability to make the right choices at the right time. It would be great if life came with a detailed set of directions. But no set of rules can replace the personal guidance of a vital relationship with God. Wisdom isn't about how smart you are, or that you always make the right choices. It's about learning to understand God's compassionate ways.

Talk to God, seek his will, ask him to bless your plans, and then commit them to his care and direction for success in carrying them out. The psalmist prays, "Teach us to number our days, that we may gain a heart of wisdom." What the mind has yet to learn, the heart already knows. God's voice of wisdom whispers to us throughout our lives, showing us the path of understanding.

No matter how many ways you seek God's guidance, in the end it comes down to making a decision, trusting that his voice will speak to your heart. Pay attention to the advice of friends, your own analysis, and the wisdom of your heart. Then you can step out in faith knowing that God is whispering in your ear, "This is the way, walk in it."

Top Ten Things to Do

10. Be open to new ideas.

9. Seek God's wisdom and guidance.

8. Make decisions that honor the heart as well as the mind.

7. Trust God will take care of things beyond your control.

6. Give yourself room to make mistakes.

5. Be grateful even for mistakes and detours.

4. Live according to your highest values.

3. Make choices out of love, not fear.

2. Remember that all things work together for good.

1. Listen for God's wisdom in every situation.

13 Practice the Presence of God

A fifteenth-century monk wrote a classic book about practicing the presence of God in daily life. Brother Lawrence meditated silently in his heart on God's love, even as he washed the monastery's pots and pans. He wrote, "I worshiped God as often as I could, keeping my mind in his holy presence."

Look for the sacred in the ordinary details of everyday life. The simple act of cooking a meal can be an offering of love. Washing dishes reminds you of spiritual cleansing. The sun on your face feels like a benediction. Look at "ordinary" things as extraordinary gifts from the hand of God.

The simplest activities can offer an experience of the sacred, if you have the eyes to see and the ears to hear. The ordinary things you take for granted can be metaphors of God's love and reminders of God's presence in your life. Practicing the presence of God reminds you that everything you do has meaning and purpose when done with prayer and dedication.

The next time you wash dishes, do laundry, mow the lawn, or sweep the floor, practice the presence of God and meditate on his greatness. Remember that greatness is hidden in humble things.

In the noise and clatter of my kitchen . . . I possess God in as great tranquility as if I were upon my knees.

Brother Lawrence

Release Your Fear to God

14

Whenever you feel afraid, take your fears and worries to God in prayer. Tell him all about it—the details that bother you, the questions you have, the losses you dread. Your heavenly Father listens to you with love and promises to guide you one moment at a time.

Fear is a thief. It steals your energy and attention—but solves nothing. You can get yourself into a complicated tangle of speculation and worry. Simplify things by choosing a serene faith in the God you cannot see, instead of the false expectations fear generates that appear to be real.

Focus on the power and greatness of a loving God who is larger than any problem or fear you may face. Speak affirming words of trust and faith, giving your worries to God instead of carrying them by yourself.

Now take that bundle of fear and anxiety and release it. Let God be in charge of it. Go on with your day and trust that you will be guided in each moment as it comes.

When fear makes you start feeling crazy, step back and say to yourself, I am fine at this moment and God is guiding me. *Break away from worry by lighting a candle, reading Scriptures, and praying aloud.*

There is no room in love for fear. Well-formed love banishes fear. Since fear is crippling, a fearful life—fear of death, fear of judgment— is one not yet fully formed in love.

1 John 4:18, THE MESSAGE

15

Embrace Change

Clinging to the past is futile. Though you might crave the comforts of what you already know, it is the nature of life to grow, evolve, and change. Human beings grow through the seasons of life, moving from childhood into adolescence and then adulthood, from immaturity to maturity.

Instead of fearing change, embrace it. Since you know change is inevitable, make changes that will improve your life. Think about your priorities and choose actions that make life easier, simpler, and happier. Whether you are getting in shape, contemplating a career change, or clearing clutter from your office, small easy actions will add up to big changes over time. Start slowly and build gently. Life is much less complicated when you don't bite off more than you can chew.

Most growth, including spiritual growth, comes gradually and often imperceptibly over time. Embracing change means that you welcome challenges and new possibilities to improve and broaden the scope of your life. Choose a deeper way of trust in God today.

To live is to change, and to be perfect is to have changed often.

John Henry Newman

Explore something that fascinates you. You may never be an astronaut, but you can always gaze at the stars. Take a class, develop a skill, and open your heart to the changes that come when you try something new.

Trust God's Timing

16

Timing is everything. Learning to trust divine timing is an art that requires patience and faith, but it bears blessed fruit. If you are experiencing delays or are frustrated because results don't come as quickly as you had hoped, take a moment to commit your hopes to God—then relinquish your need to control or predict when, where, and how things will unfold.

Accepting the limitations of human life can be an act of trust in a gracious God. It is easier to embrace life as it is than to continue resisting and rebelling. Your acceptance frees you to trust in the God who can transcend the limitations of time.

As a society we bind ourselves to time that can be measured, but God's perfect timing is rooted in eternity. Make life simpler by setting aside your impatience and cultivating trust. God's timing is like the seasons, unfolding in a higher wisdom than the human mind can understand. Trust that fruition will come in perfect ways, in God's time.

If we hope for what we do not yet have, we wait for it patiently.

Romans 8:25, NIV

The next time you are stuck in traffic or your flight is delayed, instead of complaining, look for hidden blessings. See each delay or detour as a divine appointment, knowing that God's perfect timing is at work.

17

Turn Problems into Projects

Wise choices will watch over you. Understanding will keep you safe.

Proverbs 2:11, NLT

No matter what your circumstances may be, a simple change of attitude can make them better. Making the best of a situation helps you cope with difficulties and make more of opportunities. If you've been wrestling with a problem—finances, career, relationships, health—why not take a new view of it?

Learn to view challenges as opportunities and problems as projects. Instead of defining it as a problem with all the dead-end feelings of despair, helplessness, and frustration that are attached to the word *problem*, call it a project instead. A shift in definition can inspire a shift in perspective.

A project begins with a plan. Simple action steps that are easily measurable will help you keep going when the going gets tough. A good plan offers a solution to problems and keeps you focused on your purpose and goals.

The word *project* suggests a process that leads to a positive outcome. A project is something you can work on and learn from. Ask God to help you see possibilities instead of impossibilities, projects instead of problems.

Resolve to view your problems from God's perspective. Ask God to help you discover the positive in seemingly negative situations. Then create a simple action plan that turns a problem into a project you can work on.

Clear Out the Clutter 18

Simplicity cuts through the clutter and brings order and openness to your life. If you're feeling buried under too many obligations and too much stuff, start clearing the clutter today. Buy less stuff so you have less stuff to take care of. Clear clutter on your desk or clean out a cupboard. Choose simplicity over chaos in one area, and it will eventually affect all areas of your life.

Choosing a simpler life means that you put more of your energies into creating instead of consuming. Rather than being defined by what you own, you define yourself by acts of mercy and kindness. Instead of consuming the world's resources, seek to contribute to the good of all.

Everything you have is a gift from God. Everything you give away is a gift to God. Are you willing to open your hands and release your stuff? You can start small and simply. Cleaning out a closet can inspire you to clear the clutter in a whole house. A spacious room can make you feel free.

Clean out your closet and give clothes you no longer use to a favorite charity. Cultivate a spirit of generosity by giving away something you have enjoyed so that someone else may enjoy it too.

Anyone who holds on to life just as it is destroys that life. But if you let it go, reckless in your love, you'll have it forever, real and eternal.

John 12:25, THE MESSAGE

19

Make Love Your Priority

God is love, and every step you take in the direction of love leads you straight to the heart of God. When you choose love instead of fear, you align yourself with the Kingdom of God. Choosing to serve others in love is a reflection of how God loves you. When love is your priority, you'll find your choices become simpler, less complex.

When faced with a choice today, ask yourself if you are motivated by love. Just as you are made in the image of God, so is every other person on this planet. Look at people through God's loving and forgiving eyes.

Like a tree that is planted beside the river of life, grow in God's love. Be generous with your heart and offer others compassion instead of judgment, kindness instead of indifference, and encouragement instead of criticism. Give your love freely, allowing God to bring love full circle to you again, in his own time and his own way. Share your love freely, knowing God is your supply.

> *He who is filled
> with love is filled
> with God himself.*
>
> Saint Augustine

*Express love, caring, and generosity through simple acts
of kindness. Pay for a friend's meal. Give a love
offering of time or money or personal service.
Encourage someone who is feeling discouraged.*

Challenge Your Assumptions

20

The wrong assumptions can close off options and make life unnecessarily restrictive. You can choose how you will respond to the people and situations that life brings your way. You can be closed to new ideas, or you can open your mind to embrace a larger understanding.

Don't make premature judgments and assumptions about the way things work or about your own potential. Most people thought young David was an unimportant shepherd boy, but God saw him as his loyal champion and the future king of Israel. Keep an open mind and ask God to reveal the truth hidden below surface appearances.

Choose to imagine life from God's perspective. Then you won't limit yourself to mere facts. Every time you find yourself caught up in muddled thinking, know that there is a greater truth and that anything is possible with God. Understand that your judgments and assumptions can make life more difficult. Choose an attitude of openness and humility. This opens the door to unexpected blessings and greater possibilities than you can yet imagine.

Can't you see the central issue in all this? It is not what you and I do. . . . It is what God is doing, and he is creating something totally new, a free life!

Galatians 6:15,
THE MESSAGE

Think about someone you have judged recently. Put yourself in this person's shoes and imagine what life looks like from his or her perspective. Now imagine how God looks at this person and what that means in how you treat him or her.

21   Change Your Routine

[Jesus said,] "I've come to change everything, turn everything rightside up."

Luke 12:50, THE MESSAGE

It doesn't take a cataclysmic event to change the course of your life. You can transform it one small choice at a time. It can be as simple as a change in your routine. Changing the way you do things or the way you schedule your life is a surprisingly effective way to gain a fresh perspective on what is important to you. Even a small change in what you do during the day could help you sort your priorities and become more focused.

Your willingness to change—whether it be your opinions or the way you do things—helps you grow spiritually as well. When God wants to do something new in your life, he doesn't have to overcome your resistance, but is able to guide you more easily.

Creating changes in your routine can open doors to unexpected options and opportunities. Make a small change today and develop a more flexible attitude toward life. It is better to embrace change before change is forced upon you. Life is easier when you are open to change.

Do something different. If you always drive the same way to work, try another route. If you always choose the same thing on the menu, try a new dish. Make room in your schedule for meditation or time to think.

Adjust Your Attitude

22

Just as a small change in your routine can have surprising consequences, so a slight attitude adjustment can make a big difference in the way you live your life. If you worry or make fearful prognostications about the future, the entire tone of your day is darkened by your thoughts. If you choose to walk on the sunnier side of the street, you'll find your brighter mental viewpoint colors your perspective as well.

When you choose a deep trust in God, you choose a new attitude toward life. Because you believe in a great God with great promises, you have every reason to choose a positive attitude, for he promises that all things work together for good for those who love him.

You can choose your attitude. You can allow fear to rule you. Or you can adjust your attitude and live out a fearless faith in God. Exchange your doubts for confident praise. Step out in faith. A positive attitude makes it easier to navigate life and deal with challenges that come your way.

When you have a bad day, choose to give thanks for the good things in it, even if it feels like the only good thing is that the day is over. End your day with a prayer of gratitude.

I discovered I always have choices and sometimes it's only a choice of attitude.

Judith M. Knowlton

23

Go with the Flow

The instructions of the LORD are perfect, reviving the soul. The decrees of the LORD are trustworthy, making wise the simple.

Psalm 19:7, NLT

Life is simpler if you know when to make things happen and when to let things happen. There is a perfect season for everything, a natural ebb and flow to life. You can't push a river and you can't hurry the seasons. Instead of struggling and resisting what is, relax and trust. Go with the flow of events and allow the inner wisdom of God's timing to unfold in your life.

God's timing is always perfect. Ask for his wisdom and guidance, and you will discover his divine timing in your life. He'll show you when you are ready to harvest and when you need time to allow things to ripen. You don't have to force anything, for you can rest in God's perfect timing and in his divine seasons.

You'll find that God has a better way of orchestrating your life. Unexpected encounters, delays that turn out to be blessings in disguise, and surprising solutions to seemingly unsolvable problems arise when you learn to go with the flow.

Set aside a couple of hours to let go and let God. Do something you enjoy that also gives you time to contemplate what God is doing in your life. Take a walk in the woods. Sit and daydream.

Take Time to Play

24

If you've been too busy to play, you've been too busy. We who are made in God's image are meant to play—not just when we are children but also as adults. Play revitalizes the spirit and restores a sense of perspective. Scientists talk about the breakthroughs that come when they've taken time away from the laboratory to rest and play.

Indulge your imagination, spend some time in contemplation, and enjoy simple pleasures. Make the most of small things, for this is one of the deepest joys of life. Enjoy a good book that takes you on inner adventures. Contemplate the wonders of God's creation by watching a bee browse in the heart of a flower. Savor the joy of living.

Jesus reminded his disciples that children have a wisdom that adults have forgotten. They know that play is serious business. When you relax and take a break, your imagination soars and new insights flow. So be like a little child and take time off for play.

He restores my soul;
He leads me in the
paths of righteousness
for His name's sake.

Psalm 23:3, NKJV

Mark a date and time on your calendar to do something you enjoy. Indulge in favorite childhood activities. Go to the zoo, roll in the grass, or lick an ice-cream cone. Enjoy doing something for the sheer joy of it.

Purity of Heart

The lotus flower rises pure above the mud it is rooted in, but its roots need the mud to create the luminous blossom. You, too, can flourish amid the daily cares and troubles of life when you have the clarity and courage to live by spiritual priorities.

Blessed are the pure in heart, for they shall see God. But what does purity of heart mean? It's not just keeping a list of legal dos and don'ts. Purity of heart is about simplicity of focus. It is about honoring what is most important and having the courage to live by eternal values instead of worldly priorities.

When most people think about purity, they think of untouched perfection or someone who lives above the cares of everyday life. But authentic purity is about living with clarity and purpose in the midst of the complexities of everyday life.

What do you value? Do you honor the Lord or serve yourself? Are you choosing to do good work in the world? Do you tell the truth—not only to others, but also to yourself? What kind of friends do you cultivate? Where do you spend your money? Are you willing to wrestle with difficult questions or do you prefer easy answers? How do you spend your time?

Living out your values isn't about a "spiritually correct" list of dos and don'ts. It is about living life from the heart. If you are truly honest with yourself about what you value, you will naturally make choices that reflect a pure heart.

Top Ten Things to Do

10. Pray for guidance when you are tempted.

9. Treasure loyalty and courage.

8. Be honest even in the smallest things.

7. Choose your friends wisely.

6. Do the best you can in any situation.

5. Have the courage to make difficult decisions.

4. Make wholehearted choices instead of halfhearted compromises.

3. Cultivate purity in your relationships.

2. Nurture your relationship with God.

1. Live your life with pure intentions.

25 Begin Each Day with Prayer

Each day is a new beginning. So start your day right by spending time in prayer. It will simplify your focus, setting the tone for the entire day. Ask God to help you make a fresh start. Be open to new ideas and new possibilities. Remember that you've never been here before, because each day offers a new adventure.

You will seek me and find me when you seek me with all your heart.

Jeremiah 29:13, NIV

It is good for the soul to withdraw from the busyness of life to spend quiet time alone with God. Prayer, meditation, and silence lift the heart and mind with visions of higher things. If you cultivate a regular time to meet with God, it will soon become a lifeline that offers a larger perspective of who you are and what you are meant to accomplish in life.

A morning quiet time can be your appointment to talk over the issues of your life with the God who cares for you. You might want to read Scriptures or a devotional book. This is your time alone with God, so make it special and unique to you.

Set aside a special place for morning prayer and meditation where you will not be disturbed. It could be as simple as an armchair in a corner or a quiet room with a table and chair.

Do One Task at a Time

26

Do you habitually try to do many things at once? It's called multitasking—but it can drive you crazy. When you are distracted by too many things to do, you dilute your energy. You are busy and have a great deal to accomplish. The chores are always waiting, the to-do list never seems to grow shorter. But you can accomplish more by doing one task at a time.

When you concentrate on one thing at a time, you give greater focus to your endeavors. Your list of things to do will always be there, so concentrate on what is most important and release all other expectations. Give yourself fully to one task and savor the satisfaction of work well done.

Concentrate on one task and stay focused till it is completed. Then go on to the next task. By focusing on one task or goal at a time, you harness the full energy of your mind. One thing at a time, done in simple peace, helps you accomplish more in the long run.

Instead of multitasking, give yourself wholeheartedly to one activity. Start with something simple like mending, cooking, or making the bed. Enjoy the satisfaction of completing one meaningful task without interruption.

Only eternal values can give meaning to temporal ones. Time must be the servant of eternity.

Erwin W. Lutzer

27

Be Anxious for Nothing

God is there, ready to help; I'm fearless no matter what. Who or what can get to me?

Hebrews 13:6,
THE MESSAGE

Anxiety eats away at your energy and makes you less able to cope with the challenges and problems life presents. When worry is niggling at your brain, or an unnamed fear tugs at your emotions, choose to calm your anxiety and fear by cultivating positive and faith-filled thoughts. It's a powerful way to simplify your life.

You can fritter away your energy with complaints and anxious thoughts. Use the simple tool of a Bible promise to help you remember the presence and help of the God who can sustain you in any difficulty. Cast your care on the One who cares for you.

Fear has been described as an acronym: False Expectations Appearing Real. But most of those expectations never become reality. Replace fear with the energy of faith and optimism. Trust in the big God who loves to give you, his child, the wonderful gifts of the Kingdom. Worry and fear are about the future, but faith is a choice you make right now. Strengthen your faith by exercising it today.

Just for today, replace every negative or fretful comment with a phrase of faith and optimism. Make a decision to surrender to God and commit to living your life positively and fearlessly, without reservation.

Stand in Your Integrity

28

Jesus spoke about building your house on a rock as opposed to building it on the shifting sand. Choosing honesty and integrity is like building on a rock. It is a sure foundation that will keep your feet from slipping and your enemies from hurting you.

Integrity means more than just being honest. Living with integrity means your actions are aligned with your deepest values. You speak and live the truth. You are at peace with yourself and with God. Others can trust you, knowing that you will keep your word.

Simple choices reflect integrity. Give thanks to God for the blessings you have received. Share your wealth with others and you'll have true riches. Lend a helping hand to create a warm-hearted community. Do what's right and follow God's ways.

Build your life on the rock of integrity instead of being fragmented and distracted. The simple choices of integrity are: honor your own dreams, be true to yourself, and make choices to create a life that uses your best talents and gifts.

Come and listen to my counsel. I'll share my heart with you and make you wise.

Proverbs 1:23, NLT

Decide on five areas of your life where you would like to cultivate a greater sense of honesty and integrity. Eliminate the activities, relationships, and things that drain you to make room for those that are more authentic and supportive.

29

Remember the Words of Jesus

All that belongs to the Father is mine. That is why I said the Spirit will take from what is mine and make it known to you.

John 16:15, NIV

Imagine you are sitting on a hillside above the Sea of Galilee listening to Jesus speak to the crowds. Jesus spoke of simple, human experiences like making bread, farming, and fishing, using easy-to-understand images that offer wisdom even in complex times.

Read and meditate on Jesus' words as written in the Gospels. Whether you are meditating on one of the parables—timeless stories that still resonate with meaning two thousand years later—or contemplating one incomparable phrase or sentence that brings insight for your life today, let those words be like seed thoughts that grow and flourish in your heart and mind.

Learn a phrase by heart. You'll be surprised how often those words will pop into your mind just when you need them the most. Memorization plants seeds of inspiration that will grow to full fruition in your heart and in your life. As you navigate the complexities of modern living, you'll discover healing insight that will help you stay focused on what is most important, offering timeless wisdom to guide you every day.

Enjoy reading a red-letter edition of the New Testament, where the words of Christ are printed in red. Find a passage that speaks to your heart, and meditate on it every day for a week.

Value Your Uniqueness

30

You are a beloved, unique child of God—one of a kind. God gave you special gifts and talents that you were born to share with the world. But often that vision of who you are is obscured by the wear and tear of everyday life. If you've been feeling a bit insignificant or unworthy, learn to see yourself as God sees you, and once again take your hopes and dreams seriously.

When you are working with others, don't be shy about sharing your ideas. You may be the one to offer fresh alternatives, if you value your ideas enough to share them. Be true to your deepest self, and trust that God has a purpose for your life.

Ask yourself the big questions: *Why am I here? What gifts do I have to offer the world? What is my purpose in life?* Remember that you have unique gifts and talents for making his love real in the world. Life is simpler and easier when you are true to yourself. Value your uniqueness. God does.

> *Each of us is absolutely unique and irreplaceable in the eyes of God.*
>
> Margaret Langstaff

Pull twenty images from a magazine that reflect your life or interests. Create a collage with them. What does your collage tell you about yourself? Keep the collage handy and use it as a springboard for meditation.

31

Take Time for Renewal

[Jesus] said to them, "Come aside by your-selves to a deserted place and rest a while." For there were many coming and going, and they did not even have time to eat.

Mark 6:31, NKJV

We live in a workaholic society. We are proud that we work so many hours to produce and consume more. Even though our bodies and minds need rest, we often feel guilty for taking time to sleep, relax, and simply be human. The biblical concept of Sabbath challenges the workaholic consumer society. It glorifies the beauties of the simpler life.

Create your own Sabbath rest by letting go of your frantic agendas. Instead, allow God to take care of running the universe. A nap in the afternoon sun or a brisk walk can reintegrate body, mind, and spirit. Sharing meals, taking naps, and delighting in play are all part of Sabbath renewal.

A workable strategy for remaining productive over the long haul is to balance busy times with downtime. We were created for rhythms of rest and work. God created for six days, and on the seventh day he rested. It is a simple pattern that we can use to restore balance to our own lives.

Set aside a personal Sabbath day for reflection, relationships, and renewal. Allow yourself some time to daydream, to mull over the events of the week and review priorities. Share a meal with others or play with children.

Look for Divine Appointments 32

Expect the unexpected. It may be a wonderful contact with a long-lost friend or a sudden emergency that takes you to a hospital waiting room. You may reach a long-desired goal or have to set aside a cherished dream. If you see everything as working together for good in God's time, you'll be able to see each of these unexpected events as a divine appointment.

God often brings people together in the course of their daily rounds. Paul met Lydia when he went down to the river where a regular prayer meeting was being held. Peter and John were on their way to afternoon prayer in the Temple in Jerusalem when they met and healed a man crippled from birth. A casual encounter can have life-changing effects when God is at work through his people.

When a desired outcome is delayed, look for the lesson in the detour. It is simpler to trust than to resist. Realize that each encounter is a divine appointment, each problem another opportunity for God to show you his faithfulness.

It's what we trust in but don't yet see that keeps us going.

2 Corinthians 5:7,
THE MESSAGE

Start a divine appointment journal that chronicles unexpected encounters and blessings. Write in your journal about a problem that was resolved in a surprising way, or how a seemingly chance meeting turned into an unexpected blessing.

33

Find Wisdom in Scripture

Other books are written by people for our information; the Bible was written by God for our transformation.

Terry Hall

All spiritual reading is good. But the Bible is something very special. It has nurtured the spiritual lives of millions over the centuries. From the poetry of the Psalms to the parables of Jesus, it offers illuminating words and ideas that can transform your life.

There are more than thirty-seven thousand promises to be found in the Bible, as well as history, prophecy, wisdom literature, letters, and instruction. The sixty-six books of the Bible were written over a span of hundreds of years and in different cultures and literary forms. A good Bible handbook or commentary will help you understand the background of what you are reading, helping you to get the most from the text.

If you are new to reading the Bible, buy a study Bible in a modern translation. It will help you discover spiritual riches immediately. For those who know and love the Bible, commit more time to study and meditate on its inner meaning for you. It's a rich resource for valuable insight into creating a simpler life based on spiritual priorities.

Read a chapter a day in the Bible. Or buy a one-year Bible that divides the Scriptures into daily readings. Read a chapter a day in Proverbs for a month for fresh wisdom and insight.

Seek Inner Silence

34

Take time away to meditate, pray, and quiet the chatter in your mind. Instead of listening to the noisy world around you, seek silence so you can cultivate a still place within and listen to God's voice instead. Make this a habit and you'll find that you can take the stillness with you. Then you will be able to tune in to the voice of the Spirit even in the midst of chaos.

God wants to speak to us in the silence of our hearts. When our days are too crowded to spend time with him, his heart breaks. Remember Martha and Mary? Martha was concerned with the tasks of hospitality, busy doing things for Jesus. But Mary sat at Jesus' feet, drinking in his words, just being with him.

If you set aside a quiet time for prayer and meditation, you'll discover the good God has in store for those who seek him. Once you have tasted this inner stillness and spaciousness, you'll never be satisfied with a crowded, noisy life again.

*Clear a space in your schedule for a longer silent time.
Set aside a day for quiet reflection or a weekend for
a silent retreat. Take a long walk in nature to be
with the one who created this beauty.*

*God is the friend
of silence. See how
nature—trees,
flowers, grass—grow
in silence. . . . The
more we receive in
silent prayer, the
more we can give in
our active life.*

Mother Teresa

35

Take Inspired Action

Everyone should carefully observe which way his heart draws him, and then choose that way with all his strength.

Jewish proverb

You will have more ease and joy when you invest your energy in what you love. This heartfelt way of living is worlds apart from dry drudgery or frantic fearfulness. Inspired choices made in love move you beyond frustration. A gifted musician loves the music, an athlete the sport, a teacher the learning. When you let love lead the way, you allow God's grace to support your endeavors. You'll discover that your choices of what is important to do or not to do will become simpler and clearer.

If something intrigues you or draws your attention, explore that interest. It may lead you to a whole new adventure. Trust God to find inventive ways to bring love, joy, and life lessons to you. Appreciate delightful surprises, knowing you are guided every step of the way.

Loving what you do, and doing what you love, will help you deal with obstacles and problems more easily. When you take only inspired action, you'll live life fully, in a joyful and adventurous partnership with God.

Give yourself permission to enjoy a better quality of life by investing time and energy in something you love. Create a beautiful piece of art or imagine a more effective way to serve others in your community.

Ask What Christ Would Do

36

We have it in us to be like Christ, both in character and in the way we live our lives. As he was loving, so we can be loving. As he forgave, so we can choose to forgive. As he stood for truth no matter what the cost, so we can stand for truth in our corner of the world.

God works in and through your situation and personality to bring his Kingdom into the world. Jesus offers an example to follow. Today, ask yourself, *What would Jesus do?* How would Jesus spend his time? Who would Jesus reach out to help? What would Jesus do if he met your angry neighbor? How would Jesus react to the driver who cut you off in traffic?

Think about what kind of choices you would make if you were like Christ. What would you do differently? How would you treat others? What kind of life would you lead? Just for today, do what you think Jesus would do if he were in your shoes.

To this you were called, because Christ also suffered for us, leaving us an example, that you should follow His steps.

1 Peter 2:21, NKJV

Read about and meditate on the life of Christ. Start with the Gospel of John. When others offend, pray the prayer of Christ: "Father, forgive them, for they do not know what they are doing."

Trust and Faith

Faith is a choice, not an argument. It is an inner conviction, an unshakable
assurance. Optimism is also a choice. You make a decision to trust, choosing
to believe that God will truly work all things together for good.

We can be worried people living in a troubled world. But we can also choose to be faithful people in the world that God created, orders, and saves. Though there are real dangers, it is not worry that saves us from trouble but a quiet faith in the God who delivers us and protects us.

Worry paralyzes faith, because you are assuming responsibility for things that are God's responsibility. The phrase "Be not afraid" is found more than three hundred times in the New Testament. When fear, anxiety, and worry arise, choose to trust God instead.

Choose faith over fear, for God is taking care of you and will provide for you. There are promises of protection and provision that remind you to cast all your cares on him, for he cares for you. The Bible links worry with unbelief, saying that fear is the opposite of faith. If you want to overcome worry and anxiety, learn to exercise your faith.

Find peace and serenity by choosing an optimistic faith, trusting that you will be cared for at all times. No matter what your circumstances, serenity is tied to your faith and trust in God, not what is going on all around you.

Top Ten Things to Do

10. Give thanks that you have been safely guided up until now.

9. Expect God to bring good even in difficult times.

8. Focus on possibilities instead of impossibilities.

7. Refuse to worry or be anxious.

6. Remember that faith can move mountains.

5. Choose optimism over pessimism.

4. Believe in the dawn even when it is dark.

3. Replace negative thoughts with positive thoughts.

2. See stumbling blocks as stepping-stones.

1. Believe that all things work together for the highest good.

37

Honor Your Deepest Values

Earn a reputation for living well in God's eyes and the eyes of the people.

Proverbs 3:4,
THE MESSAGE

What you become is infinitely more important than what you do or have. Even if everyone sees you as a success, you're a failure if you have to sell your soul to achieve that success. While the world may applaud outside achievements, only you know in your heart of hearts if what you are doing honors your deepest values.

It is said that reputation is what you do when everyone is looking; character is what you do when no one is watching. How do your outward choices reflect your inner values? The quiet work of God in your heart is not dictated by what you do, but by who you are. Are you becoming a better person? Does the life you live and the work you do reflect your spiritual values?

The simple life is less about outward success and more about integrity and quality of life. Caring and community far surpass outdoing others and "getting ahead." Seek quality instead of quantity, making both inner and outer simplicity a high priority in your life.

Sign a petition to support a cause you believe in. Vote in the next election. Speak up when others are afraid to speak the truth. Volunteer to help with a cause or work on a project that is important to you.

Enjoy What You Have

The appetite for more, for "new and improved!" can blind you to the riches that are in your life right now. One of the keys to simplifying your life is enjoying and appreciating what is already yours. You'll find you have riches enough here and now.

Make the most of what you already have. Use your tools to create a fun project. Decide to enjoy clothes you own but never wear. Appreciate life itself. Enjoy the beauty of creation. Appreciate your daily life too. Enjoy your home, your friends and family. Be thankful for the gifts God has given you and trust that it's more than enough right now.

Rejoice in the small things as well as the large. Look around you and see how amazing and wondrous life is. There is nothing wrong with wanting a bigger home or greater financial prosperity. All that is good. Yet God desires that you have higher aspirations, a more generous heart, and a greater awareness of the blessings you have already received.

Better a little with the fear of the LORD than great wealth with turmoil.

Proverbs 15:16, NIV

Learn to differentiate between "needs" and "wants." Instead of thinking about what you don't have, thank God for what you do have. Be thankful for the many blessings in your life. Share some of those blessings with others.

39   Cultivate Better Habits

We first make our habits, then our habits make us.

John Dryden

We are creatures of habit. Sometimes our habits do not serve us, and that's the time to ask God for help in changing them. Instead of focusing on getting rid of a bad habit, think about cultivating a positive habit in its place. Human beings respond more naturally to rewards than to punishment. Cultivate a better habit, and in the process you will naturally begin to shed the old bad habit.

Here is a simple three-step approach to changing a habit: First, make a commitment to change, focusing on what you want ("I will be more positive") instead of what you don't want ("I don't want to complain"). Second, measure your progress. For example, if you want to be more positive, observe how many times you turned a complaint into an affirmative statement. Third, keep practicing and don't get discouraged.

Good habits make life easier. You can create a habit of happiness or you can keep making choices that make you, and others around you, unhappy. Ask for God's help in cultivating good habits.

Choose one habit that needs to be changed, and a helpful habit to replace it. Commit to practicing the new habit. Put it in writing and treat it as a promise you make to God and yourself.

Be a Blessing to Others

40

·Make a conscious choice today that you will be a blessing to others. As God has blessed you, so pass that blessing on to the world around you. How can you be a blessing? You can bless others with an encouraging word or helping hand. You can also offer a silent prayer, sending prayers of blessing to each person you encounter, whether you speak to them or not.

You can bless others through practicing hospitality. Hospitality reflects the heart of God, who welcomes all into the Kingdom when they knock on the door and seek entrance. The Greek word translated as *hospitality* in the New Testament literally means "love of strangers." When you open the doors of your home, you open the doors of your heart as well.

God wants to bless the world through you. Simplifying your life makes it easier to be a blessing to others, because you are clear about your priorities and have energy to put love into action. Your acts of kindness bless others, offering tangible evidence of love.

All the believers were united in heart and mind. And they felt that what they owned was not their own, so they shared every-thing they had.

Acts 4:32, NLT

Take a moment to pray about ways you could put love into action and bless others. Make a list of five or six concrete actions you could take to demonstrate practical love. Now choose one action and do it.

41

Organize Your Day

*Order means light
and peace, inward
liberty and free
command over
oneself; order
is power.*

Henri Frédéric Amiel

It sounds simple and obvious to say that organizing your day can make things less stressful. But how many times have you missed an appointment or been late for a deadline because you were disorganized and let the day get away from you?

Take the time first thing in the morning—or last thing the night before—to plan your day. Set your alarm fifteen minutes earlier to give yourself extra time. Make a to-do list and prioritize your actions. There are many great calendars and systems for organizing appointments and schedules and for making plans. These are investments that will pay off with greater productivity and less time wasted.

As you prepare for your day, remember to offer it to God and ask for his help and blessing. Then peace will permeate your day. Creating harmony and order is worth every bit of effort, making life run more smoothly. You'll discover that being organized liberates you and simplifies your life, freeing you to focus on the things that are most important to you.

Buy a personal calendar/organizer and use it for appointments, record keeping, and daily goals. Get out of bed fifteen minutes earlier in the morning to give yourself time to make plans for the day. Begin each day with prayer.

Appreciate the Abundance

42

Appreciating life's abundance is an antidote to the constant craving for more. Choose to delight in the gifts God has already given you. Enjoy the simple things in life: sunsets, delicious food, loving friends and family, beautiful flowers, and peaceful pleasures.

Every moment of your life offers an opportunity to celebrate life's abundance. Even the mundane things of daily living, like hot water from the tap, offer simple opportunities to appreciate the works and ways of God. Human faces reflect creativity and abundance. Enjoy the view of a busy sidewalk as people pass by. God loves them all. Then take another look at your own face in the mirror, and remember that God loves you too.

Focus on the good and be grateful for all the blessings life has to offer. When you see a beautiful sunset, clap your hands with appreciation. When you hold a baby, croon your praises to the Creator. Let gratitude fill your heart as you put your energy into cultivating contentment and joy in your life.

Keep a gratitude journal to make note of the things you are grateful for right now, such as a bed to sleep in and good work to do. Each night before you go to bed, list five abundances you enjoyed that day.

Be content with who you are, and don't put on airs. God's strong hand is on you; he'll promote you at the right time. Live carefree before God; he is most careful with you.

1 Peter 5:6-7,
THE MESSAGE

43

Believe God Answers Prayer

*Cast your burden
on the LORD,
and He shall
sustain you;
He shall never
permit the righteous
to be moved.*

Psalm 55:22, NKJV

Why pray if you're afraid God won't answer your prayers? Because prayer is more than just having a celestial butler handle your requests. Prayer is communion with God. If you want things to change in your life, you need to pray, and learn to trust that when you pray, God hears and responds.

All true change comes from within, and spending nurturing time with God in prayer and meditation is the equivalent of a tree sending its roots deeper into the earth near the streams of living water. You will grow deeper in your spiritual life and see your daily life transformed in the process.

Simple faith says it's important to just be alone with God. You don't have to do anything. This is not about performance, but about being present and waiting in God's presence. Prayer changes things—but most especially, prayer changes you. No prayer goes unanswered. Pray in faith, believing that your prayers will be answered in the wisest and best way possible.

Claim Romans 8:28 (NIV) for your own: "And we know that in all things God works for the good of those who love him, who have been called according to his purpose." Write it on an index card as a reminder.

Let God Take Over

44

When you want something with all your heart, but you don't know when or if you'll receive it, you may need to relinquish it to God. You may have been struggling and praying for a long time, but after you have done all that you can do, it is up to God to do the rest. Do your best and leave the rest up to God.

When you don't know where to turn or what to do, let God take over. Let go of all you've been holding on to so tightly and put it in God's hands. This means you surrender your agenda and allow things to work themselves out. When you trust God as your source, miracles can happen. God is bigger than your biggest problem, stronger than your most frightening enemy, and greater than your doubts and fears.

Pray a prayer to let go—entrust the desires of your heart to God. Rest in his grace. Leave the situation in God's hands and know that his answer will be for the highest good of all.

Plant a seed. As you bury the seed in the soil, think of this desire of your heart and entrust it to the soil and sun. Water and nurture the plant. Its growth offers a metaphor for your faith.

The LORD will guide you continually, and satisfy your soul in drought, and strengthen your bones; you shall be like a watered garden, and like a spring of water, whose waters do not fail.

Isaiah 58:11, NKJV

45

Spend Less, Enjoy More

The consumption society has made us feel that happiness lies in having things, and has failed to teach us the happiness of not having things.

Elise Boulding

If you frequently find yourself thinking, *I'll be happy when I get this or that thing,* choose to place your happiness in God's hands. Instead of spending time longing for the things money can buy, concentrate on enjoying the things that money can't buy, including time for family, friends, and spiritual pursuits.

Instead of spending every penny you earn, cut back on expenses and live under your means. You'll breathe a sigh of relief knowing that you have some money socked away and there is more room and flexibility in your budget. Make money your servant instead of serving money.

The best things in life are free. When you look back on your life, it will be the quiet memories of meaningful moments you'll treasure, not trophies on a shelf, the size of your house, or the promotion at work. Happiness comes from the heart, not things. Trust God to satisfy your deepest needs. Then things will be in their proper place and your happiness won't be dependent on them.

Do something to make someone else happy. Enjoy the simple pleasures of giving a gift, taking someone out to lunch, meeting a need, or just spending quality time together. Remember you don't need lots of things to be happy.

Look for the Good 46

Look for the good (and God) in every situation. God is always present, even in those times when he seems far away. Though troubles may veil his presence like clouds hide the sun, he is still there.

Look for the good in yourself. Instead of looking critically at your faults, examining all your blemishes, and pointing out all your failings, learn to see yourself as a beautiful work in progress. Relax and smile at the person in the mirror. Look at yourself through the loving and forgiving eyes of God.

When the unkind behavior of others bothers you, look past their behavior to God's grace. Understand what motivates their behavior, choose how you will respond, and trust that God is at work in both of you.

Life is a sweet and precious gift from God. Appreciate the gift and thank God for the good in your life. Continually develop your appreciation through gratitude and awareness. By looking for the good, you sensitize your spirit to the hidden ways of God.

Think about a difficult situation you are facing. How might God's goodness be hiding within your troubles? Write a love letter to God, thanking him for all the gifts he has given you.

> *Surely goodness and love will follow me all the days of my life, and I will dwell in the house of the LORD forever.*
>
> Psalm 23:6, NIV

47

Lighten Up

> *If a man doesn't delight in himself and the force in him and feel that he and it are wonders, how is all life to become important to him?*
>
> Sherwood Anderson

Are you so serious about your life that you've drained the creativity and joy out of it? It's time to bring a lighthearted attitude and a more creative approach to your days. You lead a busy and productive life. Taking care of work, family, home, and all your current obligations is a more than full-time job. In the busyness of today, don't forget to make room for good times.

Always have something to look forward to. No matter how much there is to do, anticipating a coming pleasure can brighten your mood and help you accomplish today's tasks with zest.

Laughter renews your zest for life too. If you've been feeling old and cranky lately, a good laugh can lift your spirits and renew your youthfulness. Pull out old joke books or rent funny movies. Spend a few moments smiling at the antics of puppies, kittens, or anything young, awkward, and full of life. Get together with friends for laughter and good times. Lighten up and savor the simple joy of being alive.

Set up an appointment to have coffee with friends. Mark a space in your calendar to go see that new comedy that got great reviews. Do something just because it's fun and feels good to you.

Focus on God

48

When your equilibrium is upset by complications or crises, it is essential to step back, take a deep breath, and focus on God instead of on the problem. God promises to take care of you. But if you are putting all your energy into worrying about the problem, it is almost impossible to hear the still, small voice of God in the situation. Yet only God can help you navigate the problems that seem too overwhelming to deal with.

Think about the greatness of God. Contemplate the wonders of creation. How many grains of sand are there on the beach? Count the leaves on a tree. Look up at a starry sky and see eternity arching overhead. When you focus on God's immense greatness, it puts your problems into perspective.

Spend time with God to discover the peace that passes understanding. Exchange fear for faith by concentrating on the greatness of God. You may not know why the hard times happen, but you do know whom you can trust in the midst of them.

Taste and see that the LORD is good; blessed is the man who takes refuge in him.

Psalm 34:8, NIV

Meditate on Psalm 23. If the Lord is your shepherd, what does that mean in the details of your life today? Are you willing to follow the Good Shepherd and trust that he'll lead you safely?

Material Wealth

*When it comes to living out your faith, material wealth can be a stumbling block
or a stepping-stone. Love, joy, and peace are treasures that can never be placed
in a bank account, but they make life rich. Whatever your situation,
you need to appreciate and use your resources wisely.*

If you want to feel rich, just count all the things you have that money can't buy. Don't allow your net worth to determine your self-worth. You are already rich in the things that money can't buy. Money is no substitute for character or for staying true to your dreams or for bringing joy to the people you love.

Jesus cautioned against the piling up of outer things or appearances, using material wealth, social position, or worldly values to define one's self or importance in life. Enjoy material wealth, but don't allow your money and possessions to own you. Appreciate the good things you own, care for them, and share generously.

Your life should reflect the love of God first, then loving your neighbor as yourself. Give thanks for your earthly blessings, and do not despise them, but use them wisely in love and service to God and others.

Temporal things will fade away. Focus your energy and attention on eternal values. Money is not a measure of true wealth. Invest your life in things that are lasting: your children, your family, God's work, your community, and your highest ideals. You are your ultimate investment—don't settle for less than the very best that life has to offer.

Top Ten Things to Do

10. Focus your energy and attention on God's priorities.

9. Share generously with others.

8. Recognize the true value of outer appearances, knowing God looks at the heart.

7. Look for opportunities to give to God's work.

6. Invest yourself in the people you love and the community you live in.

5. Value your integrity above financial gain or social standing.

4. Be generous and share the gifts God has given to you.

3. Ask for God's guidance in money matters.

2. Thank God for all that you have been given.

1. Keep in mind that God is your source.

49

Make a Clear Choice

God is able to make all grace abound toward you, that you, always having all sufficiency in all things, may have an abundance for every good work.

2 Corinthians 9:8, NKJV

You really want to make a difference in this world, but it all seems too big for one small person to change. If you want to make a difference, there will be times you'll have to take the initiative and make a choice. Begin with one clear choice, right here and right now.

Your choices do make a difference. They count in the eyes of God, and they count in the lives you touch. A problem may seem so big that your little contribution feels like a mere drop in the bucket. But many drops eventually fill the bucket. David killed Goliath with a single stone.

Be proactive. Look at what needs to be done and start doing it. Ask God to guide you and to bring helping hands to support you. Do what you can do now. Don't focus on how little difference one small choice seems to make. You may not be able to change the world overnight, but you can make the world a better place, one little choice at a time.

Think of one problem that you've complained about. What is one practical way you can become part of the solution? Are there people you can ask to help you with this problem? Are you willing to ask for help?

Create an Affirmative Prayer

50

One creative way to align yourself with God's highest will for your life is to write an affirmative prayer. Affirmative prayer helps you express your trust in God. Speak positive words about yourself and your situation in the present tense, affirming that these things are true and that you trust God to make them true in your life.

One way to create an affirmative prayer is to personalize a Scripture verse and make it into a prayer: *The Lord is on my side, and I am not afraid.* Another way is to create a positive statement that addresses a challenge you might be facing. Here are some affirmations to get you started: My good comes to me under grace in perfect ways. Before I call, I am answered. God is my unfailing supply. I am divinely led.

Write out your personal affirmation and post it in a prominent place. Affirmative prayers can be faith builders that encourage your heart. They are simple yet bold statements that focus on God's power working through you.

Using calligraphy, write out an affirmative prayer on quality paper. Turn it into a work of art through drawing, painting, or creating a collage that expresses the essence of the prayer. Frame it as a reminder to believe.

Is prayer your steering wheel or your spare tire?

Corrie ten Boom

51

Work Wholeheartedly

Hard work is a thrill and a joy when you are in the will of God.

Robert A. Cook

Work done in the right spirit can be incredibly satisfying. It is a way to express your natural abilities and God-given creativity. When you work wholeheartedly at something, you forget yourself. Completely absorbed in the task at hand, you lose track of time and plunge into the simple pleasure of accomplishing good or making the world a better place. Whether your work is making beds and doing dishes or running a business, put your heart into your work, and the work itself will be its own reward.

You are a spiritual being, so honor the spiritual aspects of your work. Simplicity and single-heartedness are developed when you work with concentration and commitment. Focus on what is most important in each moment and release all other distracting thoughts.

Give yourself fully to one task and savor the satisfaction of work well done. Give yourself permission to do something you love with your whole heart. Perform a mundane or a difficult task that needs doing. Give it your full attention as loving service to God.

Create a harmonious workspace that enhances workflow. Make sure your chair is at the right height, the angle of your computer screen doesn't cause strain, and you have good lighting so you can see clearly.

Cultivate the Fruit of the Spirit

52

When you meet a person who is patient, kind, and loving, their looks, their social status, or the size of their bank account doesn't matter. The people who exhibit the fruit of the Spirit in their lives seem to carry a bit of God's priceless presence around with them.

Who you are and the way you live your life speaks louder than any words you can say. Ask God to show you how to make love, joy, peace, and other spiritual qualities part of your life.

For example, cultivate the spiritual fruit of love. It's good to say you love someone. But love isn't fully expressed until it's put into action. Demonstrate love practically: Take the garbage out. Offer to cook dinner tonight. Call or send a card to let someone know you're praying for him or her. One act of kindness offers tangible evidence of love. As you cultivate the fruit of the Spirit in your life you'll begin to see that life can be sweeter, saner, and more serene.

The fruit of the Spirit is love, joy, peace, patience, kindness, goodness, faithfulness, gentleness and self-control.

Galatians 5:22-23, NIV

Reflect on how you can cultivate the fruit of the Spirit in your life. Choose one of these attributes to apply to your life each week. For example, how can you be more patient with others this week?

53

Release the Past

Love does not keep a record of wrongs.

1 Corinthians 13:5, GNT

Clinging to the past is counterproductive. If you hold on to the past, you're carrying dead weight. You cannot bring the good things of the past back, and you cannot right past wrongs by obsessing over them today. Choose instead to release the past and trust God's grace for today.

Holding on to guilt and grudges steals energy from your life. Every time you complain, to others or to yourself, about what has been done or left undone, you make the wrong worse. Put the past into the hands of God, so you can live today fully. Ask forgiveness for past wrongs; forgive others for what they did to you.

Be thankful for today instead of repeating old sad stories in your mind. You'll find you have more energy to enjoy life now. Create a new story. Choose to embrace this day, trusting that God will bring even more good tomorrow. See abundance instead of loss, possibility instead of unmet expectations. Release the past with love, and rejoice in this moment.

When you catch yourself telling the old stories of loss or betrayal, stop. Ask yourself, How can I reframe this story? *Entertain the possibility that grace can turn it into a story of personal empowerment and reconciliation.*

Avoid Complaining

54

Is your glass half empty or half full? Are you concentrating on what's wrong and what you lack? Or are you looking at the good that is already available to you and trusting in God's grace—a grace that can work all things together for good? Plant a tiny seed of faith by accentuating the positive in your thoughts and conversation.

It takes more energy to resist and complain than it does to have a positive attitude. A gloomy or negative view of life is often an unappreciative one, overlooking present goodness in search of some faraway desire or longing. Cultivate contentment instead. By appreciating the riches you already have, you calm the all-too-human urge to complain about what you don't have. Look around you right now and see what treasures of contentment lie close at hand.

As you grow in the spiritual life, you'll find you have less interest in the complaint sessions that once seemed so absorbing. Look for what inspires and motivates you instead of wasting energy on trivial complaints.

The rarest feeling that ever lights the human face is the contentment of a loving soul.

Henry Ward Beecher

Take one mundane chore you tend to complain about, such as cooking meals, dusting, doing laundry, picking up after others, cleaning the bathroom, or paying the bills. Turn it into an act of love dedicated to God in gratitude.

55   Keep Your Conscience Clear

*Have a good
conscience and you
will always have
gladness; for a good
conscience is able to
endure a great deal,
and be glad even in
adversity; whereas
a bad conscience is
always fearful
and restless.*

Thomas à Kempis

Listen to your conscience. It is God's voice in your heart, guiding you to do the right thing. Keeping a clear conscience brings you a sense of inner peace, connecting you to God's grace. If you have made choices you regret, ask forgiveness and, when possible, make restitution.

As you grow in spiritual simplicity and become more attuned to the ways of God, you'll discover a greater sensitivity to right and wrong. You'll also have a more fully developed sense of authentic value. When in doubt about what to do, seek wise counsel from someone who will help you see from a higher perspective and who will tell you the difficult truths you may not want to hear. Ask God to guide you to wise counsel—and to give you the wisdom to appreciate it.

The more you listen to the guidance from your conscience, the more sensitive and accurate it will be. Then you will steer clear of dangerous temptations and frustrating distractions. And you will live a happier and more peaceful life.

*Write a letter to God about something you have had
weighing on your conscience. Write about how you
feel, your regrets, and what you would do differently.
Now burn the letter as a sign you are forgiven.*

Use Time Wisely

56

Time is a gift from God; spend it wisely and you'll be rich in the things that count. This moment is all you have. Yesterday is a memory and tomorrow is only a dream, but today is the treasure you own right now. Spend the treasure of your time wisely and you will learn to make every day a good day, no matter what the day may bring.

Time is one of your most valuable, nonrenewable resources. Instead of frantic multitasking or wasting time on nonessentials, focus on what is most important and meaningful to you. Take time to set your priorities.

Count each moment as holy. It is an act of praise and faith to enjoy the moment. Be aware of what you sense—sight, sound, scent, touch, and taste—and fully experience the here and now. Live as if each moment is a gift from God. Use time wisely, and you will taste eternity in the here and now.

How you spend your time is more important than how you spend your money. Money mistakes can be corrected, but time is gone forever.

David B. Norris

The next time you enjoy a meal with family or friends, look around the table at each loved one and savor the moment. Enjoy a better quality of life by investing time and energy in something—or someone—you love.

57   Expand Your Mental Boundaries

*Teach me your ways,
O Lord, that I may
live according to your
truth! Grant me purity
of heart, so that I
may honor you.*

Psalm 86:11, NLT

It makes a great deal of difference in your daily life what you think about God, about yourself, about others, and about how life works. Your thoughts are the starting point of your actions. God gave you an original mind, if you are willing to use it.

So many people settle for hand-me-down ideas. You may have a limited idea of yourself or what is possible. But new ideas can transform a world—whether it is the new product that creates a market or the new concept that frees an individual. You have a limitless God who has created you to be a limitless thinker. Cultivate that gift by being open to new ideas and possibilities.

If you think negative or limiting thoughts, you will make choices that lead to a more limited life. If you think expansive thoughts of faith and trust, you'll find a richer, more expansive life follows. You can train your mind to think in more expansive ways. Thoughts are the building blocks of your experience. Build well.

*Investigate educational offerings in your area:
community colleges, special courses, private lessons,
etc., and choose something that you think would
be fun to take. Challenging yourself with classes or
workshops keeps you from getting stuck in a rut.*

Eliminate Nonessentials

58

Are you feeling overwhelmed? It is easy to be sucked into false urgencies, whether by panic-inducing headlines or an overwhelming list of things that must be done before the end of the day. Focus on what's really essential. Ask yourself these questions: *Do I consider the activities I engage in to be worthwhile? Will this simplify my life or make it more complicated? Is this something I love to do?* If many of the activities you engage in seem superfluous or onerous, it's time to look at what's most important to you.

Do not be afraid to say no to that which does not serve your highest purposes. Even good things can be distractions from the higher calling and purposes of God for your life. Know and respect your limits.

Ask for God's guidance to help you eliminate the nonessentials. Go away to a quiet place and listen to whispers of eternity. You will find grace, peace, and wisdom to keep you balanced when the urgencies of life would unbalance you.

Make wise choices that simplify your life by focusing on quality instead of quantity. Learn to differentiate between "needs" and "wants." Instead of thinking about what you don't have, thank God for what you do have.

Those who weep or who rejoice or who buy things should not be absorbed by their weeping or their joy or their possessions.

1 Corinthians 7:30, NLT

59

Acknowledge the Blessings

Blessed is he who has regard for the weak; the LORD delivers him in times of trouble.

Psalm 41:1, NIV

When times are tough and you're not sure how you're going to get through them, take a minute to acknowledge the help you have received. Parents, pastors, teachers, friends, mentors—you've been helped by many people. Appreciate the gift and thank the giver. Continually develop your appreciation through gratitude and awareness.

Cherish your family and loved ones. They will not be here forever and neither will you. Take time to really see how beautiful and unique each person is and remember what he or she means to you. Focus on the good and be patient with the less than perfect.

Remember the blessings and thank those who have helped you in the past. Honor them for the gifts they have given you: a helping hand, an encouraging word, a stirring example. Focus on the help you've received instead of the needs you still have. When you look back at how God has provided for you, it will inspire you to believe that God will provide for you again.

Send a thank-you note to someone who helped or encouraged you. Resolve to create a community of giving and receiving. Start by helping a friend or neighbor, and don't be shy about asking for help in return.

Focus on Quality and Value

60

The seductive voices of the consumer society urge you to overspend. But what use is a houseful of things you don't enjoy and never use? Did you really need another pair of shoes or the latest electronic gadget?

If you have a choice between several cheap items or one quality item for the same price, don't be fooled into thinking that quantity makes up for quality. One beautifully made piece of clothing will serve you better than five cheaper items of lesser quality. Make wise choices that simplify your life by focusing on quality instead of quantity—in relationships as well as in material things.

How many times have you settled for clutter and noise when, with minimal effort, you could have had beauty and order instead? Learn to discern true quality in every situation you encounter, whether it is a fine piece of furniture or a friend worth knowing. Learn to know when enough is enough. Instead of buying more things or stuffing your personal schedule with too many activities, simplify your life.

Any intelligent fool can make things bigger, more complex, and more violent. It takes a touch of genius—and a lot of courage—to move in the opposite direction.

E. F. Schumacher

Buy a fine-quality tool that will serve you dependably for many years. Instead of cluttering your closet with trendy clothes that will go out of date, enjoy a few classic pieces that will serve you through the years.

Blessings and Gratitude

One of the easiest ways to cultivate inner simplicity is to practice gratitude. By giving thanks for what you receive, you are able to enjoy and share even more of the good gifts of life. You begin to realize that you are rich in the blessing of God's love.

If you are reading this page, you are already blessed, with much to be thankful for. First of all, you are breathing. You are alive. You have received the mysterious and wonderful blessing of life as a human being.

Next, God's presence is with you, here and now. There is no place you can go where God is not. It is your choice to receive or reject his presence in your life, but his presence always goes with you.

If you picked up this book, it was because you have an interest in leading a simpler life. But it is also because you have an even deeper desire to create space in your life for greater blessings, and the greatest blessing of all is knowing God more intimately, removing every bit of clutter that keeps you from experiencing his loving presence in your life.

You have eyes to see this page and the skill to read these words. See how simple blessings can be? Yet, like the gift of life itself, these everyday blessings, often taken for granted, are rich with mystery and wonder. Now realize that every moment is filled with blessings, and every day you are alive is a gift to be grateful for.

Top Ten Things to Do

10. Appreciate every moment for the gifts it brings.

9. Learn to see the blessings in everything.

8. Share gifts and blessings with others.

7. See the blessings in plain and simple things.

6. Cultivate a more intimate relationship with God.

5. Practice contentment and contemplation.

4. Express your gratitude for everyday blessings.

3. Realize life is rich with wonder and mystery.

2. Remember that God is always with you.

1. Thank God for the gift of life.

61

Identify Your Patterns

He who reigns within himself and rules his passions, desires, and fears is more than a king.

John Milton

Just as clearing clutter from your living space calms and soothes the soul, so being aware of your emotional clutter helps you make better choices that help you live life more freely from the heart. Old patterns can include the stories you tell yourself, as well as the ego agendas that trip you up in your relationships.

Perhaps you have a pattern of looking at life through the lens of lack. You tell yourself stories about what you don't have, or why people don't really care. But are those stories really true? It is empowering to look at your patterns from a higher perspective so you can see the pattern of limited thinking, and choose a different mind-set.

How you think about your life can make a big difference in how you experience life. If you always focus on what you don't have and what is wrong, you will create more stress through your frustration and negativity. Instead, choose to focus on what's right and good in your life. Create a happier pattern for living.

The next time you find yourself opening your mouth to defend a decision you made, stop and think. Don't waste energy in self-defense. Be willing to admit your errors, look for ways to improve, and move on.

Go on a Retreat

62

No matter how busy you are or how many obligations you need to fulfill, you also need to renew and replenish your spirit. Consider going away for a day, a weekend, or even a week for personal or communal retreat. If you can't get away, prescribe an hour of personal renewal at home. Take a long, hot soak in the tub or curl up with a good book. Let this be a time to meditate on the events of your day and to ask for God's guidance tomorrow.

[Jesus and his disciples] left by boat for a quiet place, where they could be alone.

Mark 6:32, NLT

Time away with God is a vital necessity. A retreat—personal or with a group of fellow spiritual seekers—offers an opportunity to view your life from a higher perspective.

Jesus left the crowds behind and went to the wilderness to pray. Spend time away in God's creation. Seek serenity of spirit through time away in prayer, solitude, and intimate moments with God. Remember that you are a human being, not a human doing. Set aside time for rest, retreat, and prayer.

Take a miniretreat during a busy day. It's vitally important to give yourself simple time-outs for stress relief. Escape from the office for a brief walk. Drink a glass of water or fruit juice. Meditate for a moment.

63 Allow Others to Help You

God has given us two hands—one to receive with and the other to give with. We are not cisterns made for hoarding; we are channels made for sharing.

Billy Graham

You may believe that you should be strong and self-sufficient all the time, and that it is weak and shameful to ask for help. But in God's economy, it takes both giving and receiving to create a balanced life. When you give too much without receiving, you become exhausted and depleted.

Make life easier by learning to receive as well as to give. Ask for help when you need it, without guilt or shame. Let people know that you need help, advice, or encouragement. Do not be attached to their answer. If they say no, trust that it is because someone else is the right person to help. Don't turn help away because of feelings of unworthiness. Accept help with joy.

Know that what goes around comes around. Pray for those who have helped you, trusting that God will bless them in ways you cannot imagine. Just as you have delighted in helping others, so allow others to delight in helping you. Put false pride aside and allow God to send you his ministering angels.

When you are feeling overwhelmed, make a list of people you can call on for help or encouragement. Reach out to one person on that list today. Remember that receiving is as important as giving, and allow others to help you.

Be a Cocreator with God 64

Creativity is your birthright. We are made in the image of God and when we create we honor that which is most holy and sacred within us. Everyone was meant to live creatively. Preparing a tasty new dish, planting a garden, writing a poem, creating a window display, singing a song, decorating an office, sewing a doll's dress, building a tree house—you express yourself, and God's very nature, through creative choices.

Tap into the spiritual energy of divine creativity. Let your creative choices be inspired, coming from deep within. Make God your friend, partner, and cocreator. Ask for inspiration and guidance. Trust that you are being guided as you work one step at a time to bring a creative dream to fruition.

Ephesians says that we are God's "poems"—works of creation in progress. God was pleased with his creation of the world as chronicled in Genesis. Allowing yourself to be creative reflects a similar joy in God's creativity. God created you in his image—and you reflect that image back through your creative partnership with God.

Seek first the
kingdom of God
and His righteousness,
and all these things
shall be added to you.

Matthew 6:33, NKJV

It is not by spectacular leaps that we move more deeply
into creativity, but by slow, incremental steps. Set aside
regular time for practicing and nurturing your
creativity. Build skills with simple daily repetition.

65

Say Yes and Mean It

You don't make your words true by embellishing them with religious lace. . . . Just say "yes" and "no." When you manipulate words to get your own way, you go wrong.

Matthew 5:34-37,
THE MESSAGE

Have you found yourself getting tangled in easy promises that are never going to be put into action? When you are torn between pleasing another person and being true to yourself, do you often find you have given them an answer you think they want to hear instead of speaking straight from your heart?

While it's important to be helpful and to avoid offending others, it is essential to be true to yourself. If someone wants you to help with a good cause, but you know it will take more time than you can give, it's better to say, "No, I can't help at this time," than to make a halfhearted promise that you know you can't possibly keep. You won't let people down, and you won't feel guilty for not keeping your word.

Letting your "yes" be "yes" and your "no" be "no" can be a powerful way to live in clarity and peace. You'll know you mean what you say and will follow through, staying focused on what is most important.

Just for today, watch your speech and commit to telling the whole truth and nothing but the truth. No making excuses, embroidering the facts, or waffling between "yes" and "no." Commit to the truth and stick to it.

Cultivate Authentic Happiness

66

Gifts of happiness are always available. The essence of the simple life is found in practicing the art of contentment. God scatters the seeds of life's little wonders, pleasures, and joys throughout your day. Small gifts like fresh flowers, hugs, sunshine, birds singing, and friends and family who love you are sources of authentic happiness and quiet joy.

Happiness is a choice. It's a matter of attitude as much as anything. Decide to like what you get instead of demanding that you get what you like. Live as if each moment is a gift from God. You can say to yourself, *I choose to be happy in this moment, to be content with simple things.*

Authentic happiness does not depend on big events or monumental achievements. It comes from the daily blessings we often take for granted. If you have food, shelter, and good work to do, you are rich. Harvest happiness from life's simple blessings. Then think about how you can multiply the harvest of happiness by sharing these gifts with others.

You show me the path of life. In your presence there is fullness of joy; in your right hand are pleasures forevermore.

Psalm 16:11, NRSV

Set aside some time to enjoy simple pleasures. Dig in the garden, take a walk, or work on a creative project. Do something you enjoy that also gives you time to contemplate what God is doing in your life.

67

Let Go of the Old

Obsession with self in these matters is a dead end; attention to God leads us out into the open, into a spacious, free life.

Romans 8:6,
THE MESSAGE

Our lives are cluttered with too many things. We become attached to nonessentials, unable to pass them on even when they are no longer useful to us. The more we hoard, the greater number of things there are to clean, maintain, and take up space in our homes.

Make room in your life and create space for something new by releasing material things you've been holding on to for too long. Release and bless that which no longer serves you. Give away what you can no longer use.

How often have you clutched at the status quo, fighting the natural forces of change, trying to control and confine life within the small boundaries of your fears and expectations? Move beyond rigid opinions and limited ideas. Let go of old attitudes that no longer serve you, and release old expectations and disappointments. Open your heart and hands to receive God's gifts of grace. Only by letting go and letting God can you find the simplicity, joy, and freedom that were always meant to be yours.

Give away things that have been sitting in boxes and never used. Weed out the clutter, and keep only that which feels useful or beautiful. Pass the good along to others to make room for new blessings.

Share Generously

68

A generous heart finds simple joy in giving. By sharing good things with others, you loosen your tight grip on the things that perish and place them in God's hands instead. As you give, you will receive.

Develop an inner spirit of generosity by giving something away. Give your best, not a discard. Buy a gift that you would enjoy receiving or share something that has held meaning for you. Give the gift of yourself, along with the thing you give away. Giving in this generous spirit frees God to give you more, for he knows you can be trusted with his good gifts.

Like a tree that is planted beside the river of life, grow in God's love. Be generous with your heart and offer others compassion instead of judgment, kindness instead of indifference, and encouragement instead of criticism. Give your love freely, allowing God to bring love full circle around to you again, in his own time and his own way. Share your love freely, knowing God is your supply.

Give, and you will receive. Your gift will return to you in full—pressed down, shaken together to make room for more, running over, and poured into your lap.

Luke 6:38, NLT

Cultivate a spirit of generosity by giving away something you have enjoyed so that someone else may enjoy it too. Write a check to support a cause you admire. Contribute your time to a charity you believe in.

69

Move in a Positive Direction

Well-spoken words bring satisfaction; well-done work has its own reward.

Proverbs 12:14,
THE MESSAGE

Sometimes a desired goal may feel like an unachievable target, far beyond your strength and ability. But a wall is built brick-by-brick, and a goal is reached step-by-step. You may think you have to make spectacular leaps, but baby steps are the surest way to reach your goal. Just as a bricklayer patiently adds one brick at a time to the wall he is building, so one positive action after another will help you create your dream.

It takes faith and courage. Yet each simple step leads to the next step. Give yourself credit for even small goals accomplished. You would celebrate a toddler's first steps. So celebrate even a simple baby step of faith, knowing it will lead you where you need to go.

Take your plans, hopes, and dreams to God in prayer. Trust that he is using every situation to bring you closer to your goal, even when setbacks occur. God is with you, so take another positive step in the direction of your dreams.

Hold a minicelebration for a goal you accomplished or a personal victory. Call a friend and say, "I did it!" Treat yourself to a small reward and celebrate your accomplishment before you move on to the next task.

Give Thanks in All Situations

70

Happiness depends on favorable outer conditions. You receive a bonus or promotion, you can afford a special vacation, or it's a perfect sunny day. But seasons can change, and instead of sunny skies, rain falls. A devastating loss, illness, and difficult times seem to bring no reason to rejoice.

That's when you need to go to the source and find your joy in the Lord instead of circumstances. He will be your comforter and provider. Even in the darkest night, he can bring joy in the morning. Take your fears and worries to God, and give thanks for his care.

You can waste a lot of energy fighting hard facts. When times are tough, practice gratitude for the unseen grace that is always with you. This attitude of gratitude helps you relax your resistance and accept the current of grace that flows within your life. Giving thanks will help you find serenity in troubled times and become more aware of life's precious gifts in all seasons of life.

Be thankful in all circumstances, for this is God's will for you who belong to Christ Jesus

1 Thessalonians 5:18, NLT

When fear makes you start feeling crazy, step back and say to yourself, I am fine at this moment and God is guiding me. *Instead of talking about what you don't have, express gratitude to God for every blessing.*

71

Refrain from Anger

If you are patient in one moment of anger, you will avoid one hundred days of sorrow.

Ancient proverb

How much energy do you waste on anger? What good does it do for you to hold a grudge against someone who hurt you? The answers to these questions may seem obvious, but our emotions often cloud the issue, making forgiveness seem counterintuitive and holding a grudge the most natural thing in the world.

Anger is fueled by a habitual way of looking at the world. Anger can be a pattern of behavior, a choice of thoughts, and an attitude toward life. Ask yourself what triggers your anger. You'll probably find the person or circumstance that sets you off is different every time, but the pattern of your behavior is always the same.

Instead of nursing anger in your heart, ask God to show you how to transform your rage into a passion for peace and patience. Inner peace is a skill that is honed over time by the choices you make, whether it is choosing to refrain from anger or taking time every day to seek inner calm in the presence of God.

Today, make a commitment to choose peace and forgiveness. Write the name of someone you need to forgive. Now tear up or burn that piece of paper as a physical manifestation of your decision to forgive and release your pain to God.

Cultivate Purity

72

Fresh air, purified water, organic veggies, and clean living are a cliché in all the books and articles on simple living. It is good to cultivate purity in the things you eat (no junk food!) and clear away clutter in the home you live in. But there are other levels of purity that make you feel even more alive.

Maintaining personal purity is a spiritual choice that affects your well-being. Your entertainment choices color your mood and affect your attitude. Choose entertainment that lifts your spirits and activities that encourage you to be a better person. Spend time with friends who honor your values and encourage you to be your best.

When you haven't lived up to your ideals, remember that purity of spirit can also be found in a love that covers a multitude of sins. While you cannot change your past choices, you can cultivate the purity of heart that comes from God's love and forgiveness. Choose the highest good in everything you do and be pure in heart and intention from now on.

Pure motives will make a clear flame. Impure motives are the smoke that clogs the flame.

Sidney Cook

When you want to watch something on TV, look for programs that inform as well as entertain. Choose uplifting movies with great stories instead of movies with thin plotlines and violent special effects.

Spiritual Disciplines

Throughout Christian history, various spiritual principles, disciplines, and practices have aided believers in a quest for deeper knowledge. What has worked for other believers can help you grow in your faith and develop a vital relationship with God, promoting faithfulness and regularity in spiritual practice.

How do you know what God wants you to do? How can you go about making decisions that honor the Lord? The spiritual disciplines offer a way to stay in constant communion with the divine presence.

Begin with spiritual reading. In his book on spiritual reading, *Take and Read*, pastor and writer Eugene Peterson observes, "Spiritual reading does not mean reading on spiritual or religious subjects, but reading any book that comes to hand in a spiritual way, which is to say, listening to the Spirit, alert to intimations of God."

Make Bible reading a regular part of your day too. A few minutes of reading in the morning can set the tone for the rest of the day.

Meditation is a quietly powerful way to deepen your spiritual life and draw closer to God. Cultivating stillness helps you become more open to the Spirit's influence.

Prayer time is not another obligation to fulfill. It is a sweet appointment to meet with God, to tell him about your troubles and triumphs, to praise and worship, and to ask for help. There are many other spiritual disciplines that can help you cultivate the inner life. From service and giving to study and prayer, these disciplines deepen your walk with God.

Top Ten Things to Do

10. Set aside a time for daily meditation.

9. Read the Bible and spiritual books on a regular basis.

8. Nurture intimacy with God.

7. Keep a spiritual or prayer journal.

6. Learn about the spiritual disciplines.

5. Affirm trust in God with words of faith.

4. Set aside time for prayer, praise, and worship.

3. Contemplate the meaning in the daily events of life.

2. Have a teachable heart and a childlike attitude.

1. Be still and listen to God.

73 Use Financial Resources Wisely

Here's the lesson: Use your worldly resources to benefit others and make friends. Then, when your earthly possessions are gone, they will welcome you to an eternal home.

Luke 16:9, NLT

Use your resources wisely. Finances can be a stumbling block—or a stepping-stone. Honor your obligations and take care of business. Instead of spending every penny you earn, cut back on expenses. Pay bills promptly. Make money your servant instead of serving money.

Set money aside for savings. Having savings available gives you peace of mind during times of unexpected trouble. It also means that you are free to say yes to unexpected job opportunities or take care of needs that arise during times of financial stress. Seek out information and expert advice to help you safely navigate financial waters.

Set a portion of your money aside for planned giving that acknowledges God as the source of your wealth. Don't let your net worth determine your self-worth. Remember that you are already rich in the things that money can't buy. Money is no substitute for character. Remember that you are your ultimate investment—don't settle for less than the very best that life has to offer.

Watch for small expenses that can add up quickly. Cut out that expensive daily latte for a week and you'll save money. Lowering expenses can feel like getting a raise in pay!

Be Patient

74

Green apples need a time of ripening before they become fully red and ready to eat. You can pick them early, but all you'll end up with is a sour taste and an upset stomach. Be patient and wait till the fruit is ripe. It's easier in the long run to wait until the timing is right, whether with fruit or with the circumstances of your life.

Replace worry and anxiety with trust and faith. When you have given a concern into the hands of God, leave it in God's hands. You can choose your attitude in this moment. Patience is the secret power of the faithful heart. The life of faith calls for an inner simplicity that depends on grace, not on human willpower.

God's timing is always perfect. Ask for his wisdom and guidance, and you will discover his divine timing in your life. You need time to grow in grace and maturity. You don't have to force anything, for you can rest in God's perfect timing and his divine seasons.

Practice patience with people you encounter during the day.
For example, pray for others when you are stuck in traffic,
or let others go ahead of you in line at the grocery store.

> *Think of farmers who*
> *wait patiently for the*
> *spring and summer*
> *rains to make*
> *their valuable crops*
> *grow. Be patient like*
> *those farmers and*
> *don't give up.*
>
> James 5:7-8, CEV

75

Take Minibreaks for Vitality

*Take one long breath
to help you relax and
relieve tension and
stress. Deep breathing
has a positive, long-
range impact on
your health.*

Zig Ziglar

When your day feels hectic and out of control, it's vitally important to give yourself simple time-outs for stress relief. Escape from the office for a brief walk. Drink a glass of water or fruit juice. Renew your energy with exercise.

Breathe deeply. Take a gentle deep breath, feeling it reach down toward your tummy. Exhale it with an audible sigh. Did you feel your body relax as you exhaled? In the Bible, the words for spirit and breath are often interchangeable. As you notice your body's breath, remember to breathe in the love and energy of God's Spirit.

Remember to take frequent stress breaks during a busy day. Take a few minutes for prayer, for exercise, for hydration, and to regain perspective. Take a break. Sit. Stare. Do nothing. Stop and look up to watch the clouds move across the sky, and allow your heart and mind to rest in God. Including minibreaks during the day can refresh your body, renew your perspective, and replenish your spirit.

*Use a simple deep-breathing exercise as an opportunity
to pray. Sit up straight and take a long, deep breath.
Breathe in the love of God. Exhale and let go
of that which no longer serves you.*

Be a Fully Alive Person

76

When was the last time you met someone who approached life with zest and joy? Can you remember how it felt to be in his or her presence; how that person brought a special zing that made life seem exciting and worthwhile?

Are you fully alive? Do you celebrate the life God has given you—rain or shine? Open your senses to the wonders of creation. Enjoy spending time with friends. Embrace the gifts each day brings. Be open and receptive. Choose to greet each moment with the enthusiasm of a child.

When you relax into God's grace, you will discover that every day can be a good day. To be fully alive means that you don't have all the answers, because life is larger and more wonderful than you can yet imagine. When you say yes to life, you are saying yes to the unknowns. The unknowns are where the growing edge is, where life and creativity are most fertile and abundant. Be fully present in the miracle of this day.

The glory of God is a human being fully alive.

Saint Irenaeus

When you're feeling old and jaded and tired, become like a child again. Take off your shoes and wiggle your toes. Move your body freely and joyfully. Clap your hands. Sing and praise God spontaneously.

77

Enjoy Simple Pleasures

I think there is an art of simplicity. It will need no end of thinking out, and it is worth learning.

Temple Gairdner

Gifts of happiness and joyful pleasures are waiting for you, if you are willing to look for them. God scatters the seeds of life's little wonders, pleasures, and joys throughout your day. It doesn't take much to make life feel abundant and rich. A simple thing like a pair of new socks, fresh flowers, or a seat in the bleachers can make the simple life feel extravagantly luxurious with little outlay of cash.

Take a fifteen-minute "life appreciation" break. Reconnect with what you loved as a child and refresh your spirit. Indulge in a favorite dessert. Buy crayons and a coloring book and color to your heart's delight. Simple childhood pleasures remind you of essentials of the heart and infuse adulthood with creative joy.

This kind of happiness does not depend on big events or monumental achievements. It comes from the daily blessings we often take for granted. If you have food, shelter, and good work to do, you are rich. Harvest happiness from daily living and enjoy life's simple pleasures.

Appreciate the little blessings of daily life. Think about how you can multiply the harvest of happiness by sharing these simple gifts with others. Pick a bouquet of flowers, bask in the sun, and celebrate the simple things.

Release Perfectionism

78

It's one thing to love excellence. It's another thing to drive yourself crazy attempting to be perfect. Perfectionism is another way of trying to control life. But life is much larger than your limited ideas of what it should be.

Artists know that perfection is not all it's cracked up to be. It takes a little chaos, some crazy mistakes, and a few detours to make an interesting piece of art. Soulless mass production is no substitute for the freshness and vitality of the human touch, the unique fingerprint on a creative project.

In the beginner's mind, there are endless possibilities. In the mind of the expert, there are a limited number of answers. Instead of rigid resistance, relax and go with the flow. Look for ways to turn a less-than-perfect situation into the right situation for you. Instead of complaining, ask God to show you how to make things better. Drop the baggage of unmet expectations and open yourself to the serendipities of life. Allow the divine perfection of grace to surprise you.

Lord, let me know my end, and what is the measure of my days; let me know how fleeting my life is.

Psalm 39:4, NRSV

Celebrate the grace of "imperfection": A cherished antique. Small children and mud pies. A happy tail-wagging dog. Start a painting and deliberately make a "mistake" on the canvas. Now see what perfectly imperfect picture you can create.

79

Create a Simple Action Plan

Commit your way to the LORD, trust also in Him, and He shall bring it to pass.

Psalm 37:5, NKJV

Whether you are getting in shape, contemplating a career change, or clearing clutter from your office, small easy actions will add up to big changes over time. Simple action steps that are easily measurable will help you keep going when the going gets tough.

Evaluate your present goals in light of what you love. Set a goal that lifts your heart with anticipation. Then create a simple and doable action plan. A plan is a container for grace. You create a plan, and God helps you see it through. Make manageable plans. Giant leaps can be scary, but baby steps are doable. Small, incremental changes are less intimidating and will take you over the long haul. Life is much less complicated when you don't bite off more than you can chew.

Planning helps you focus your efforts and energies, and offers a way to measure what you've done and how far you've come. Whether you plan a day or a month, a good plan keeps you focused on your purpose and goals.

Make a monthly plan to bring more balance, serenity, and simplicity into your life. List goals you want to reach and break them out into small action steps. Include room in your plans for the unexpected.

Forgive and Move On

80

A friend lets you down. You're the victim of a crime. Someone you trusted betrays you. You have a choice: forgive or keep holding the grudge. If you hold on to bitterness and resentment, you hold yourself hostage to the past. If you choose to practice forgiveness, you set yourself free from the past and give God room to heal the pain.

Practicing forgiveness is not easy. People say and do hurtful things that can't be unsaid or undone. However, with God's grace, they can be forgiven. Forgiveness is a two-way street. We all need forgiveness. The God who forgives you will give you the grace to forgive others—and yourself—if you truly desire it.

When you choose to forgive, you give a great gift to yourself as well as to the other person. You give the gift of freedom. No longer bound by the past, your choice to forgive opens a door to the future. When you forgive others, you open your heart to God's love and create a place for healing to begin.

Try this exercise when you need to forgive yourself. Look directly into a mirror and say out loud to your reflection: "God forgives you, and I forgive you. God loves you, and I love you too."

He that cannot forgive others breaks the bridge over which he must pass himself; for every man has need to be forgiven.

Thomas Fuller

81

Release Your Resistance

I will walk in freedom, for I have devoted myself to your commandments.

Psalm 119:45, NLT

Sometimes life feels like a wrestling match. You've struggled and struggled to solve a problem or reach a cherished goal, yet never seem to overcome the difficulty or achieve your heart's desire. What gets more results—praise or criticism? People respond to praise, while constant criticism eventually discourages them from even trying. Do you criticize yourself and create inner resistance?

You can waste a lot of energy fighting what is. You may be sick or have financial limitations. Your job might not be as fulfilling as it once was. Beating yourself up is useless, for what you resist, persists. Accepting that these conditions exist is not admitting defeat. It is acknowledging what you have to work with. Yet grace can transform a situation in surprising ways.

Resist or surrender—it's your choice. Relax into the freedom of grace. Surrender your disappointment to God. Allow room for creative responses to arise instead of holding on tightly to either-or scenarios. When you have faced and accepted what is, you open the door to new possibilities.

Pay attention to your inner dialogue. Do you judge yourself harshly when you make mistakes? Choose loving and encouraging thoughts instead. Relax and learn to laugh at yourself, knowing you are a work in progress.

Pare Down Your Schedule

82

You expend energy every day. Work demands your best effort, people need your attention, and chores pile up like autumn leaves. You dream of a simpler life, but the complications of everyday living get in the way.

If you've been burning the candle at both ends, it's time to cut back on some of your activities. There are so many worthwhile activities; it's hard to say no, because you don't want to miss out on any good thing. Yet if you become sick and unable to meet your obligations, you have no choice but to clear your schedule. So do it now before your body rebels.

Simplify life by paring down your schedule. Make having free time and getting enough rest a higher priority, and you will be rewarded with greater energy, clearer thinking, and a more relaxed attitude toward the ups and downs of life. You'll be less likely to make mistakes or overlook important details. For a happier life, create a schedule that balances busy times with quiet time.

Speak, move, act in peace, as if you were in prayer. In truth, this is prayer.

François Fénelon

Clear your schedule for a quiet evening at home. Make yourself go to bed at least one hour early. You'll find the extra rest will help you wake up more refreshed in the morning.

83

Choose Optimism

He who earnestly seeks good finds favor, but trouble will come to him who seeks evil.

Proverbs 11:27, NKJV

Optimism can be cultivated by an act of faith. Faith is a choice, not an argument. It is an inner conviction, an unshakable assurance. Every day you are faced with decisions. You must make choices. You can choose to respond negatively or positively to the ideas and situations that God brings your way. You can choose an optimistic attitude toward life.

Every thought you think colors your experiences, so choose your thoughts carefully. Negative thoughts that hold us back include: *I can't. I won't. It's not fair. It won't work. It's too hard. I'm not good enough.* Optimistic thoughts help us make positive choices. Choose to replace negative thoughts with positive, empowering thoughts like: *I can. It's possible. I'll give it a try. I am able to do this. I can make this work.*

Focus on what is good in your life. Wash the windows of your soul by asking God to cleanse your thoughts every day, replacing negative defeatist thoughts with positive affirmations of faith and hope.

For just one day, consciously choose to replace every negative comment with a positive comment. Watch your thoughts too. Are they critical or gloomy? Exchange those negatives for something more hopeful and positive.

Unplug and Recharge

84

The six o'clock news offers a litany of war, horror, corruption, greed, and trouble. The front page of the newspaper details the latest scandal. The media offers a constant flow of chatter, opinion, and advertising. Though it's important to know what's happening in the world, you also need time to listen to your spirit.

Consider going on a media fast for a few days. Instead of watching TV, spend time in prayer and meditation. Ration your media exposure. Pull the plug on the electronic chatter for a day or even several days. Turn the radio off and let the silence soothe you.

Let go of all the chatter and opinions and to-do lists; just be with God in the silence. Allow the silence to fill you and expand your thoughts. Savor the sound of birdsong, or listen to the wind rustle the leaves in the trees. Take a nap. Go for a walk in the woods or on the beach. Silence refreshes your spirit, allowing you to hear whispers of eternal love.

*I've cultivated
a quiet heart.
Like a baby content
in its mother's arms,
my soul is a
baby content.*

Psalm 131:2,
THE MESSAGE

*Declare a media fast for twenty-four hours. Instead of
listening to the radio as you drive, turn the talk and music
off and enjoy the quiet. Set a schedule for reviewing
e-mail instead of constantly checking for messages.*

Prayer and Presence

*Prayer is communion with the God who loves us. You can come to
God in prayer at any time, any place. He wants to be intimately involved
in your life. When you pray you enter God's presence and
discover that God has been present with you all along.*

Prayer begins with deep listening, waiting on God, entering into his presence. It is a way of being open to a more intimate relationship with the divine. Practicing the presence of God is a path or a spiritual process, helping, as the Bible would say, the "word to become flesh." By praying, meditating, listening, and being present, then acting on what we have heard, we can create a larger life than we once thought possible.

To develop a quality of prayerful presence in our lives, we must begin by stilling the disjointed judgments and chatter of our minds, calming our emotions so we are free to move from conventional thinking to a more spiritual viewpoint.

We can choose to move beyond the time-bound limitations of a stressed-out lifestyle to enter into the timeless and eternal. Whether it is fifteen minutes of silence and quiet meditation in the morning or a weekend retreat, this withdrawal from the noise and stress of the daily grind is essential to our spiritual growth.

"Peace, be still!" Jesus said to the stormy Sea of Galilee, and the seas calmed to glassy stillness. So we also learn to calm the storm of our emotions and thoughts to enter the quiet place of prayer.

Top Ten Things to Do

10. Create a time and space for meditation and prayer.

9. Let go and let God run the universe.

8. Give thanks for all things.

7. Worship and praise with your whole heart.

6. Make prayer a priority in your life.

5. Be aware that God is always present.

4. Enter into the silence.

3. Come to prayer with an open heart.

2. Remember that God loves you.

1. Be still and know that God is here with you.

85

Sleep on It

Sleep re-creates. The Bible indicates that sleep is not meant only for the recuperation of a man's body, but that there is a tremendous furtherance of spiritual and moral life during sleep.

Oswald Chambers

A calm spirit in a rested body is a beautiful thing. Are you getting enough sleep or are you up at all hours? If you're tired, frazzled, and overcommitted, it's time to cut back on your busy schedule and make time for some much-needed rest.

It's easy to get caught up in a fast-paced lifestyle and forget to take care of your own needs. Refresh yourself with a quick nap. It can be a brief catnap in a chair or a real lie-down with comforter and pillow on your bed. If you're especially tired, set aside time for a longer, deeper nap. Remember that naps are not just for children—grown-ups need them too.

As you rest your body, you renew your spirit. Hours of sleep before midnight are more rejuvenating, so an earlier bedtime can pay off in greater energy during the day. If you are not getting enough sleep, decide to modify your habits. Make restful sleep a priority and you'll reap both energetic and spiritual benefits.

Take a catnap in the middle of the day to refresh yourself. Make sure you have a cozy comforter and favorite pillow ready for naps. Wrap a quilt around you and relax into its warm softness.

Seek New Ideas

86

There are unlimited possibilities for someone with an open mind. Don't settle for hand-me-down ideas that no longer fit today's circumstances. You may have a limited idea of yourself or what is possible. But new ideas can transform your life. You have a limitless God who created you to be a limitless thinker. Cultivate that gift by being open to new ideas and possibilities.

If you think you have all the answers, you don't even know what the questions are. Limited thinking means limited options. Learn to cultivate the quality of curiosity in your life. It takes courage to be willing to try something new. You have to be brave enough and want it enough to make the attempt.

An open mind is liberating. Though you might crave the comforts of what you already know, it is the nature of life to grow, evolve, and change. Embracing new ideas means that you are open to God bringing you fresh opportunities and new possibilities.

No one can be making much of his life who has not a very definite conception of what he is living for.

Henry Drummond

Make a deliberate choice to be flexible in body as well as mind. Take a class that stretches you—whether it's an exercise class or learning a new skill. Actively look for new ideas and ways of doing things.

111

87 Forgive Yourself

You were forgiven by God long before you knew you needed forgiveness. Now it's time to take those promises of grace seriously and forgive yourself. You made choices and you cannot unmake them. But you can make better choices if you forgive yourself and walk on in God's grace.

God made you in his image. You are unique, and God loves you. Knowing that God loves you and has called you to participate in his creative work frees you to forgive yourself. As you forgive yourself, you are more able to forgive others.

Mistakes, loss, errors, and failures are often the fertile compost that helps you grow a better life. A toddler keeps getting up after falling because she's determined to walk. She concentrates on where she's going, not where she's been. So you can learn from your errors and move beyond them. Ask for forgiveness, and never waste energy in guilt, self-justification, or regret. Instead, simply accept forgiveness and move on.

Commit to a fresh start. Instead of criticizing yourself, encourage your heart with praise and gratitude for God's immeasurable forgiving grace. Remember that God loves you and forgave you even before you asked.

Put God First

88

If you have felt far away from God lately, who moved? Renew your commitment to following God and putting him first. Make a decision that can change your life profoundly: the decision to seek after God and follow wherever he takes you.

One way is to begin the day with prayer before the busyness of another day rushes in. In the freshness of a new day you can come to God with a rested mind and a heart clear of all distractions. You give him the best of your time. When you pray before you begin your day, you tune your soul to God. Then your day reflects the inner harmony of that precious time of morning prayer.

When you choose to put God first, with no holding back and no reservations, get ready for some wonderful changes. Old habits that no longer serve fall away. Attitudes will shift; priorities will change. When God is at the center of your life, the rest of your life will order itself around him.

We make our decisions, and then our decisions turn around and make us.

Francis Willliam Boreham

Mark this date in your journal or calendar as the day you decided to follow God with all your heart. Write about what putting God first means to you. List practical ways to put God first in your life.

89

Pray without Ceasing

God is always with you, always listening, already present in this moment. You can talk with the Lord about your troubles, praise him in your moments of triumph, and share small pleasures that make you grateful to be alive. Sense God's presence in the daily round of the life you live now, and this simple choice will bring a new focus and clarity to your days.

Nothing is too great and nothing is too small to commit into the hands of the Lord.

A. W. Pink

Whatever each moment brings, meet God there and include him in whatever you are doing. God is ever present, so pray without ceasing. When you cultivate an awareness of God in each moment, you bring fresh meaning to daily tasks and affirm that it all matters to God. Then each moment of your life becomes a prayer.

A loving relationship with God makes each day more meaningful and precious. Every decision you make is colored by your relationship with God. Complex problems find spiritual solutions. Every conscious choice becomes a prayer that says yes to joy and clarity. Life becomes simpler when it's bathed in prayer.

Approach everything you do as a partnership with God, including him in even the most mundane tasks. As you get ready in the morning, be mindful of God's presence. Let washing, dressing, and eating be a celebration of praise.

Practice Common Sense

90

Common sense has been defined as wisdom dressed in work clothes. You learned simple commonsense wisdom when you were a child: Say thank you. Share your toys. Be kind to others. Trust God. Be content with what you have.

This homespun heart-wisdom still applies, no matter how sophisticated your adult world seems to be: Give thanks to God for the blessings you have received. Share your wealth with others and you'll enjoy true riches. Lend a helping hand to create a warmhearted community. Do what's right and follow God's ways. Honor these simple truths and you will be blessed.

God is the source of all wisdom, and he says in the Bible that he will give wisdom to anyone who asks for it. By cultivating a regular relationship with God, you will find that his wisdom helps you see beyond surface appearances, giving you what you need to handle every circumstance. If you have found yourself longing for commonsense wisdom that can help you find solutions in life, just ask God.

Fine sense and exalted sense are not half so useful as common sense.

Alexander Pope

Take time to enjoy a conversation with someone you admire. Ask what simple truths have guided him or her through life. Pray each morning for God's wisdom on how you can best use your time that day.

115

91

Watch Where Your Money Goes

*Get wisdom—
it's worth more
than money;
choose insight
over income
every time.*

Proverbs 16:16,
THE MESSAGE

How you spend your money reveals what you believe more accurately than you realize. Your spending reflects whether or not you believe God provides for you. Look at your spending habits and evaluate whether they serve you or impoverish you.

Do you overspend? Do you pinch pennies and deny yourself because you are afraid you won't have enough to see you through? Watch where your money goes and you'll see your motivations and true beliefs revealed. What you spend and how you spend tell you a lot about who you are and what you believe.

When you are feeling worried about finances, consider giving a special offering. Giving is an act of faith. Give cheerfully and willingly, for God rewards a generous heart in his own time and in his own way. Sow seeds of faith that remind you God can meet all of your needs. Let the law of sowing and reaping work in your favor by giving freely and generously to life.

*Be aware of how much you spend and where. Track your
spending in a notebook for the next week. Look at where
your money really goes and decide if your spending
habits reflect your spiritual priorities.*

Be Proactive

92

Initiative is doing the right thing without being ordered to do it. You have to step up, step out, and get involved if you want to have an impact on life. Weigh your options, ask God for wisdom, and then take the first step. Do what you can with what you have, and be willing to take the initiative by being proactive.

By taking the initiative instead of waiting for someone else, you create the change you want to see in your life. Don't let fear of failure stop you. Successful people are proactive, initiating what they want to accomplish without prodding or procrastination. Whatever the outcome, you'll learn something new and valuable.

Second-guessing, trying to control outcomes, or playing it safe can be deadening to the spirit. Take risks and trust God. Go ahead and do something you want to do but are afraid to try. See this as a grand new adventure, with God as your friend and companion along the way. Be proactive and leave the results in God's hands.

The LORD your God will bless you in all your harvest and in all the work of your hands, and your joy will be complete.

Deuteronomy 16:15, NIV

Write out your goals for this week, this month, and for the coming year. Make sure each week includes doing something toward achieving longer-term goals. Stop procrastinating and start a project that is important to you.

93

Trust the Truth to Set You Free

If you hold to my teaching . . . you will know the truth, and the truth will set you free.

John 8:31-32, NIV

Jesus Christ embodied truth—showing us the reality beneath the appearance of things. When you are struggling to distinguish truth from illusion, listen to what God has to say about the situation or question. Let him speak to your heart, then stand in the truth you have been given.

When difficult situations arise and lies seem to be prevailing over truth, place your trust in the promise that the truth will set you free. Like Christ, choose to embody the truth, believing that God will guide you safely through illusions and lies into liberating reality.

Others may doubt or disagree with what you believe. Listen respectfully to what they have to say. Then listen to your own heart. If your beliefs differ from theirs, be loving and respect the differences between you and others. Choose a deeper trust in God and focus on the truth as you understand it. By choosing to live in hope and to stand in your truth, you are making a statement of faith in God.

Remember a time in the past when the truth set you free. What did you do when others disagreed, and how did you want to act in this situation? Now speak your truth and trust you will be set free again.

Give Your Best Effort

94

In the Kingdom of God, even the most mundane work can be blessed service. Take pride in giving your best, knowing that you work for God, not for human beings. See all work as sacred and your job as not just work, but as ministry. Bring more love to what you do. Do your work in the right spirit. See your career as a vocation, a calling from God. Do your best work and trust God to take you to the next level tomorrow because you did your best work today.

The returns you experience will reflect the effort you put into realizing your goals. If you've skimped on the details, it will show in the final product. Be faithful in the small things, and God will bless and prosper your work. A fine craftsman puts integrity into every detail of his work and it shows. Do whatever it takes to make something right. Lay a strong foundation by paying attention to details, taking pride in what you do, and giving it your best effort.

Give yourself permission to be passionate about life—whether it is a glowing interest in art, sports, or business, or a passion for spiritual understanding. Authentic passion is an expression of praise to God.

Pay careful attention to your own work, for then you will get the satisfaction of a job well done, and you won't need to compare yourself to anyone else.

Galatians 6:4, NLT

95 Let Grace Be Your Strength

*Trust the past to
God's mercy, the
present to God's love,
and the future to
God's providence.*

Saint Augustine

Grace is a gift of God, bringing humanity into the mercy, freedom, and love of God. The former slave trader John Newton wrote the hymn "Amazing Grace," saying, "'Tis grace hath brought me safe thus far, and grace will lead me home."

When life is complex and you have difficult choices to make, find clarity and simplicity by trusting that grace will be with you whatever you decide. Grace is God's answer to your cry for help. His forgiveness is given freely through Christ. Accept the love that answered before you called and offer that same grace to others.

If you are attentive, you'll find reminders of grace everywhere. You can see God's gifts of grace in the beauties of creation and the marvelous variety of people and how they express their unique gifts. Let God's grace be your strength at all times. Grace is a gift freely given by a loving God. Cultivate an awareness of grace every day and you will find comfort in all seasons of life.

*Be kind in the way you speak to yourself. Instead of
calling yourself "stupid," be gentle and say you are
"God's child." You are beloved by God, so let your
words and attitude reflect that fact.*

Learn from Your Mistakes

96

Everyone makes mistakes. But the greatest mistake you can make is to refuse to learn what they can teach you. When you are willing to learn from your mistakes, you no longer need to define them by what went wrong but by the lessons they taught you so you could do better.

Mistakes are the construction zones of life that make you slam on the brakes and ask yourself, *What's going on here?* They are reminders that everyone, no matter how young or old, is a work in progress. Mistakes can lead to unexpected solutions. For God to complete his work in your heart, you have to be willing to risk making mistakes and to learn from them, no matter where you are on life's journey.

Mistakes are part of the process. Learn from them. Like a child who stumbles learning to walk, pick yourself up and keep on walking. Then, instead of complicating life with guilt and regret, you start afresh and live more spontaneously.

There is precious instruction to be got by finding we were wrong.

Thomas Carlyle

Realize that you win some and you lose some. Laugh at some of your mistakes. Enjoy the process, viewing mistakes as opportunities to learn and grow instead of disasters to deny or defend.

Harmony and Order

Timeless simplicity soothes the spirit, creating an oasis of calm in a busy life.
Make a commitment to clean up, clear out, and bring order into your life.
Your soul responds to beauty. Your spirit needs space. Order and
harmony are the hallmarks of a life of simplicity and joy.

Outward actions like cleaning the house, making do with less, and creating beauty in your surroundings are balanced with inner choices that help you remember what is most important and meaningful to you. As you simplify, you make room for personal transformation and spiritual growth.

Harmonious surroundings take advantage of clean lines and natural beauty. Life is much easier when your living space is clear of clutter and filled with beauty and light. An ordered living space seems to give you more room for creative thinking. You will breathe a sigh of relief in the pristine order and harmony you have created.

Create an oasis of restful cleanliness and serenity in your home. Things run more smoothly when the house is freshly cleaned and the atmosphere is lightened by your elbow grease. Use your housecleaning time to put your thoughts in order too.

Open a window and get some fresh air. Put some calming music on the stereo. Set a bouquet of fresh flowers on a table. Enjoy a nourishing meal. When you create more harmony and order in your life, you'll find that you have more energy to focus on the things that are important to you. You'll live harmoniously in body, mind, and spirit.

Top Ten Things to Do

10. Clear the clutter.

9. Bring order out of chaos.

8. Open the windows for fresh air.

7. Calm the mind and listen to God.

6. Make home a restful oasis.

5. Keep things neat and clean.

4. Order your priorities for simpler living.

3. Create harmonious surroundings.

2. Nurture your soul with beauty.

1. Cultivate inner harmony and peace.

97

Meditate on God's Character

Meditate within your heart on your bed, and be still.

Psalm 4:4, NKJV

Think about what it means to be like Christ. Meditation offers a quietly powerful way to get to know God more intimately. From the psalmist who meditated on God's law and character, to Mary, the mother of Jesus, who pondered all things in her heart, the Bible teaches the value of time spent in meditation. Jesus told us to go into a private place for an intimate encounter with God. Meditation and prayer bring your life into alignment with his nature.

We have it in us to be like Christ, both in character and in our relationships with one another. As he was loving, so can we be loving. As he forgave, so we can choose to forgive. As he stood for truth no matter what the cost, so we can stand for truth in our corner of the world.

Think about what kind of choices you would make if you wanted your life to reflect God's character. What would you do differently? How would you treat others? What kind of life would you lead?

Use a simple reminder, such as a phone ringing or a bird singing, to prompt a moment of prayerful thought in your day. Meditate on the character of God and how you can express that in your current situation.

Choose Friends Carefully

98

If you want a simpler and happier life, choose your friends with care. Avoid whiners and complainers. Spend your time with friends who encourage you. Invest your time with people who maintain a good attitude and have a positive outlook on life.

Sometimes you have to let go of friends who lead you astray. Friends are very influential in your life, and some may drag you down to their level. They may not be bad people, just bad for you. You may need to walk away from toxic relationships, whether it is the buddy who tempts you to unhealthy ways or someone who is always criticizing you.

Choose friends who are inspiring to be with—people who love God and who want to live in ways that make the world a better place to be. You can become especially close to friends who share the spiritual journey. These are the friends who encourage you to reach for the highest and best within you, and who lead by their own good examples.

Think about your friendships. Who lifts you up and makes you feel better? Who drags you down and makes you feel bad about yourself? Make a list of friends you enjoy spending time with and call one today.

A friend is called a guardian of love or, as some would have it, a guardian of the spirit itself.

Saint Aelred of Rievaulx

99

Honor God's Purposes

We are His workman-ship, created in Christ Jesus for good works, which God prepared beforehand that we should walk in them.

Ephesians 2:10, NKJV

You don't have to be rich or famous to have a positive impact on your world. No one else can do what you can do, be what you can be. Never underestimate the potential of the partnership between you and God. He planted the life force within you, and you were born to reach for the stars. Eternity is in your heart, so trust in that and aim high.

Commit to honoring God's purposes in your life. Choosing a simpler life frees you to follow his guidance and fulfill your destiny. God wants to bless others through you, and because you're here, you can trust he has a purpose for your life. Ask God to guide you, and he will show you how to be a blessing to the world.

Honor God's call on your life every time you make an important decision. Ask yourself if this decision will serve the highest good. Remind yourself that you are somebody special in God's eyes, called to a unique and wonderful path of growth and service.

Find inspiration in heroes and role models. Read a biography of a famous man or woman who answered an unusual call from God (e.g., Corrie ten Boom, Albert Schweitzer, Thomas Merton, Elisabeth Elliot, Dietrich Bonhoeffer).

Sow Seeds of Faith Today

100

A tiny black seed holds the potential for leaves, flowers, and fruit when it's planted in rich soil, watered, and cultivated. A simple prayer holds the same creative power when you plant it in the soil of faith and tend it with love. When you have a mountain to move, start by planting a seed prayer.

It doesn't have to be complicated. Make your request known to God. Then thank God that the answer is coming, even though you may not yet know how. Make a marker in your garden of faith, and then give it time to grow in God's grace.

It is good to affirm your faith on any day, but especially valuable to affirm faith on a day when doubts cloud your mind. God rewards faith. Sow in faith and trust that one day you will reap in joy. Wait patiently like a farmer who has sown seeds, letting God bring your prayer to quiet fruition in his good time. A strong faith makes a simple life more meaningful and fruitful.

Write down an affirmation of faith on a small card and carry it in your pocket or purse. It can be a Scripture verse or a personal affirmation, such as "I am guided by God."

I learned really to practice mustard seed faith, and positive thinking, and remarkable things happened.

Sir John Walton

Don't be obsessed with getting more material things. Be relaxed with what you have. . . . God assured us, "I'll never let you down, never walk off and leave you."

Hebrews 13:5, THE MESSAGE

Let your gentleness be known to everyone.
The Lord is near.

Philippians 4:5, NRSV

Don't store up treasures here on earth, where moths eat them and rust destroys them, and where thieves break in and steal.

Matthew 6:19, NLT

The kingdom of God is within you.

Luke 17:21, NIV

Sin is no longer your master, for you no longer live under the requirements of the law. Instead, you live under the freedom of God's grace.

Romans 6:14, NLT